D1799277

WORKBOOK

CAE result!

KATHY GUDE

OXFORD

OXFORD
UNIVERSITY PRESS

Great Clarendon Street, Oxford OX2 6DP

Oxford University Press is a department of the University of Oxford.
It furthers the University's objective of excellence in research, scholarship,
and education by publishing worldwide in

Oxford New York

Auckland Cape Town Dar es Salaam Hong Kong Karachi
Kuala Lumpur Madrid Melbourne Mexico City Nairobi
New Delhi Shanghai Taipei Toronto

With offices in

Argentina Austria Brazil Chile Czech Republic France Greece
Guatemala Hungary Italy Japan Poland Portugal Singapore
South Korea Switzerland Thailand Turkey Ukraine Vietnam

OXFORD and OXFORD ENGLISH are registered trade marks of
Oxford University Press in the UK and in certain other countries

© Oxford University Press 2006

The moral rights of the author have been asserted

Database right Oxford University Press (maker)

First published 2006

2010 2009 2008 2007 2006
10 9 8 7 6 5 4 3 2 1

No unauthorized photocopying

All rights reserved. No part of this publication may be reproduced,
stored in a retrieval system, or transmitted, in any form or by any means,
without the prior permission in writing of Oxford University Press,
or as expressly permitted by law, or under terms agreed with the appropriate
reprographics rights organization. Enquiries concerning reproduction
outside the scope of the above should be sent to the ELT Rights Department,
Oxford University Press, at the address above

You must not circulate this book in any other binding or cover
and you must impose this same condition on any acquirer

Any websites referred to in this publication are in the public domain and
their addresses are provided by Oxford University Press for information only.
Oxford University Press disclaims any responsibility for the content

ISBN-13: 978 0 19 457728 1
ISBN-10: 0 19 457728 7

Printed and bound by Grafiasa S. A. in Portugal

ACKNOWLEDGEMENTS

The authors and publisher would like to thank Tom Bradbury, Petrina Cliff,
and the advanced students of EF International Language School, London.

The authors and publisher are grateful to those who have given permission
to reproduce the following extracts and adaptations of copyright material:

p4-5 abridged extract from 'Better and Better' by Caroline Righton from *The
Guardian* 23 April 2005 © 2005 by Caroline Righton. p8 abridged extract from
'What are friends for?' by Jenni Russell from *The Guardian* G2 24 January 2005
© Guardian Newspapers Limited 2005. p10-11 abridged extract from 'Sled
Time Story' by Jenny Diski from *The Observer* 30 January 2005. Reproduced by
kind permission of AP Watt Ltd on behalf of Jenny Diski. p17 abridged extract
from 'Now NASA looks to change Earth into a garden of Earthly delights' by
Robin McKie from *The Observer* 28 March 2004 © Guardian Newspapers
Limited 2004. p21 abridged extract from 'The Power of Darkness' by Hugh
Wilson from *The Guardian* 15 March 2005 © Guardian Newspapers Limited
2005. p24-25 abridged extract from 'Take The Plunge' by Dottie Monaghan
from *Woman and Home* magazine © Woman and Home/IPC & Syndication. p28
abridged extract from 'The Animal Olympics' from *The Daily Express* 11 July
2005 © Express Newspapers 2005. p29 abridged extract from 'Among The
Giants' by Sebastião Salgado from *The Guardian* 7 May 2005. Reproduced by
kind permission of the author. p30 abridged extract from 'Human Body Has
No Limits, Says Texas A & M Professor' from the website www.tamu.edu.
Reproduced by kind permission of the author. p34 abridged extract from 'Out
to Lunch' by Bibi Van der Zee from *The Guardian* G2 24 January 2005 ©
Guardian Newspapers Limited 2005. p36-37 abridged extract from 'I need a
heroine' by Tanya Gold from *The Guardian* 1 July 2005 © Guardian
Newspapers Limited 2005. p41 abridged extract from 'Giant mirror to light
up village' by Barbara McMahon from *The Guardian* 14 September 2005 ©
Guardian Newspapers Limited 2005. p44-45 abridged extract from 'Is This
The Death Of The Big Easy?' by Peter Sheridan from *The Daily Express* 3
September 2005 © Express Newspapers 2005. p48 abridged extract from
'Great Tales From English History Volume 1: From Cheddar Man to the
Glorious Revolution' by Robert Lacey used by permission of Little Brown, an
imprint of Time Warner Book Group UK, and Curtis Brown Group Limited.
p50-51 abridged extract from 'We're funny in the brain' by Jerome Burn
from *The Times* 30 October 2004 © The Times 2004. p56-57 abridged extract
from 'Families and other criminals' by Suzanne Yager from *The Telegraph*
April 2005 © Daily Telegraph 2005. p60 abridged extract from 'Tough Love'
by Rebecca Smithers from *The Guardian* 21 June 2005 © Guardian Newspapers
Limited 2005. p64-65 abridged extract from 'The Tiger's Teeth' by Jonathan
Watts from *The Guardian* 25 May 2005 © Guardian Newspapers Limited 2005.
p71 abridged extract from 'The biggest flatpack table and chair ever' by Dan
Carrier from *Camden New Journal* 16 June 2005. Reproduced by kind
permission of the author. p76 abridged extract from 'Feel-good factor but will
it save the planet?' by John Vidal and Paul Brown from *The Guardian* 20 May
2005 © Guardian Newspapers Limited 2005.

SOURCES:

p40 www.bodyoptimise.com

p61 Review of Ocean's Twelve by Mark Dujsik from www.mark-reviews-
movies.tripod.com

p69 'Free Enterprise' by Donnie Walker from www.bbc.co.uk

p74 'Learn about modern art periods' from www.soyouwanna.com

p81 'Battle of the bag' by Caroline Williams from The New Scientist 11
September 2004.

*The publishers would like to thank the following for their kind permission to
reproduce photographs:*

Alamy pp10/11 (Bryan & Cherry Alexander Photography), 15 (Andrew Morse),
20b (Bryan & Cherry Alexander Photography), 28bc (blickwinkel), 28bl (Walt
Stearns/Stephen Frink Collection), 35r (Popperfoto), 44/45t (Nick Higham), 70
(Shangara Singh), 76bl (David Gordon), 80 (Pictor International/ImageState),
93tl (Ian Miles-Flashpoint Pictures), 94cl (John Powell Photographer), 96br
(Popperfoto), 96tr (Henry Westheim); Corbis UK Ltd. pp11 (Setboun), 14 (Paul
A. Souders), 16l&17 (NASA/Roger Ressmeyer), 21 (Images.com), 24/25 (Mark
M. Lawrence), 25 (Stephen Frink), 26l (Bill Ross), 26r (Anders Ryman), 28tc
(Abbie Enock/Travel Ink), 28tl (Kevin Schafer), 28tr (Tom Brakefield), 29 (Tim
Graham/Sygma), 35l (Helen King), 36b (Sunset Boulevard), 41 (Ray Juno),
44/45b (Bettmann), 45r (Philip Gould), 47 (Ludovic Maisant), 49r (Keren Su),
50 (©LWA-Stephen Welstead), 51 (Simon Marcus), 60 (John Henley), 72 (Tom
& Dee Ann McCarthy), 74r (Burstein Collection), 75 (Darama), 76t (Gideon
Mendel), 92cl, 92cr (China Photo/Reuters), 92l (Jim Bourg/Reuters), 93br
(Roger De La Harpe/Gallo Images), 93tr (Michael Freeman), 94bl (Tom
Stewart), 94br (David Pollack), 94cr (Eric K. K. Yu), 94tl (Tom Stewart), 94tr
(James Leynse), 96bl (K.M. Westermann), 96tc (Helen Atkinson/Reuters), 96tl
(Frank Trapper); Empics p92r; Getty Images pp5 (Karen Moskowitz/The Image
Bank), 9 (West Rock/Taxi), 20t, 46; Guardian Newspapers pp8l&r (Linda
Nylind 2005); iStockphoto pp52 (Tomaz Levstek), 64l (Daniel Brunner), 64/65t
(Stefan Klein), 74l (Dave White); Linographic pp64/65b, 69(all); Mary Evans
Picture Library p48/49; NASA pp16c (Pat Rawlings), 16r (Mark Dowman/John
Frassanito & Associates); Orion Publishing Group p57; Oxford University
Press pp27, 40l; Photolibrary pp28br (Mary Plage), 34, 76/77 (Peter J.
Robinson); Rex Features pp48t (Fletcher), 54 (David James); Ronald Grant
Archive pp36c (Warner Bros.), 37, 40r, 61, 93bl; Still Pictures p81 (Emmanuel
Vialet); Transworld Publishers Ltd p56.

Illustrations by:

Gill Button pp13, 53; Melvyn Evans pp19, 33, 59, 73, 79

Researched illustrations by:

Oliver Gaiger pp7, 39, 66, 67, 68; David Tazzyman/ PVUK pp30-31

What are you like?

Reading Part 3 Multiple choice

1 Read the article quickly and decide which sentence
   (a, b or c) is the best summary.

   a Dealing with problems in your life.
   b Finding out how to take things easy.
   c Learning to be more positive.

2 Read the text again and choose the correct answer
   (A, B, C or D) to questions 1–5.

   1 What does the writer advise people to do before
      getting up in the morning?

      A Calmly contemplate their day ahead.
      B Organise their routine to maximise their time.
      C Decide which undesirable activity they could
         dispense with.
      D Reject the idea of having to fulfil their
         obligations successfully.

Better and **better**

TAKE A COUPLE OF MINUTES to lie still in bed and
reflect on the day ahead. Do you feel cheerful or
fed up, excited or bored? Or do you, perhaps, feel
nothing? Go on, prod your subconscious to consider your
5 situation. Unless you get pleasure from living a passive
and non-eventful life, having a non-committal attitude
can actually be as bad as being pessimistic. So if, as you
walk yourself through the events of the day ahead, you
feel pretty average about things, then try and aim higher.
10 It will mean that you get much more out of life. So there
you are, lying in bed. Picture yourself showering, making
breakfast, catching the bus, attending meetings,
shopping, cooking supper, watching TV and finally getting
into bed. Did your spirits sink at the thought of any of it?
15 If so, pluck what it was out of the timetable and examine
it more closely. Is it a must-do, non-negotiable event? For
instance, you may not mind the idea of going to work but
hate your job or the daily commute. Find out what
options you have to make changes or find alternatives. In
20 the meantime, come up with a strong and confident
affirming statement about the person you wish to be and
the way you wish to tackle these life challenges.

Once you have a clear picture of the things in your life
that make you feel low, either eliminate, minimise or
25 improve them and the way you manage them. If getting
everyone organised in the morning is a nightmare, you
need to apply some lateral thought to the process.
Encourage everybody to help with the morning routine.
Make everyone responsible for some parts of their own
30 organisation. If everyone is leading busy lives in the
household, it makes no sense for one person to be a
martyr. Be realistic about your own stamina and stress
limits and appreciate the importance of keeping yourself
fit and happy. Agree new regimes with family members
35 or housemates as a sensible training exercise, and stick
with it until everyone takes their equal share. Instead of
feeling miserable about your chores and responsibilities,
adopt a positive approach and acknowledge that they are
an essential component of life.

2 The writer suggests dealing with difficult aspects of our home lives by

   A freeing up more time to handle them more effectively.
   B delegating some responsibilities to others.
   C learning to control stress by taking more exercise.
   D asking for outside help to relieve pressures.

3 The writer initially implies that adopting a realistic attitude towards life can

   A have a counterproductive effect on our lives.
   B encourage us to look on the bright side of life.
   C enable us to find solutions to our problems.
   D help us be more analytical in our approach to life.

4 The writer justifies having a positive outlook on the day by saying it will

   A make the outcome of our day more predictable.
   B help us blank out the less desirable events in our lives.
   C give us renewed energy to face up to problems in life.
   D reinforce our appreciation of what makes life worthwhile.

5 According to the writer, how should we react to having had a bad day?

   A Focus on the one positive thing that happened, however insignificant.
   B Try to communicate our feelings about it to another person in a positive way.
   C Tell ourselves it is perfectly acceptable to feel down after a day like that.
   D Stay positive and believe that tomorrow will be a better day.

40 Pessimism, doubt and negativity can often disguise themselves as realism. Facing up to the facts can sometimes be healthy but it's essential not to poison hope and optimism with negative thoughts. Observing how you think is vital. You really need to tune into 45 hearing those negative waves as soon as they start and see a more positive alternative view. To find this perspective, you may need to examine closely the experience or subject of your attention. Be curious and interested in life, the things and the people that make 50 up your day. Be resolute that you will find a positive in everything and everyone.

The logical rationale for having a positive attitude is compelling. Nobody knows for sure what each day will bring and whether its end will mark a personal triumph 55 or disaster. Make yourself work out what good things will happen. Today could be the day you meet your soul mate, or when you are praised or promoted. Carry a list and photographs of things in your life that are rewarding or make you feel happy. This can include loved ones, 60 favourite flowers, song tracks, a cutting from a newspaper that made you laugh, or a theatre ticket that reminds you of a wonderful occasion. If you need reminding that good things do happen, take this collection out and relive fond memories and thoughts.

65 Even if today has been a bad day, you needn't go to bed depressed because your optimism didn't pay off. Why? Well, because tomorrow is another day. In the same way that a single look or a sour comment can instantly kill a feeling, so a bubble of optimism arising from even the 70 most minor triumph will eventually get bigger if you refuse to let yourself look on the dark side. That is the great thing about life.

Vocabulary

Feelings

1 Put these words into a suitable category below. Then use them to complete sentences a–g.

▪ depressed confident cheerful fed up
curious pessimistic resolute optimistic
moody realistic

Positive: ....
....

Negative: ....
....

Neutral: ....
....

a I'm .... with everyone asking me to do things for them all the time. Nobody ever says thank you or helps me.

b Bob has a rather .... attitude towards the future of our planet. He's convinced global warming will destroy the planet very soon.

c We must be .... and do everything possible to improve the transport facilities in the town.

d Zeb seems very .... He wasn't nervous about making that speech to the whole college.

e You're not being very .... about our plans for the summer. We just couldn't afford to go on holiday to a place like that.

f You never know how Ann will feel – happy, sad – she can be very ....

g I'm .... to know how many students passed the exam, aren't you?

Meanings of *get*

2 Match the expressions in italics in a–h with one of the meanings in brackets.

a If you want to *get more out of* life, try to be more organised. (create or invent more from/extract or obtain more from)

b I'd like to *get out of* going to the party tonight but I don't see how I can. (avoid doing something/ persuade someone not to do something)

c I'm really struggling with this grammar. I just don't *get* it. (understand/like)

d We ought to be going home. It's *getting on for* midnight. (past/nearly)

e It's no good *getting* upset about what happened. There's nothing you can do about it now. (making/becoming)

f The students *get on with* each other very well. (make progress/have a good relationship)

g I think it's time we *got down to* doing our homework. (finished/began)

h This argument is *getting* us *nowhere*. Let's just agree to disagree. (achieving nothing/leading us in the wrong direction)

3 Complete sentences a–g using a suitable expression with *get* in the correct form.

a Do you .... with Kate? I really don't know her.

b We need to .... doing all the jobs in the house that we haven't done for ages.

c This consultation process is .... It's virtually impossible to please everybody.

d It's .... 6 o'clock. Great! It's nearly time to finish work and go home!

e I want to try to .... college, you know, join some clubs or learn a new language.

f Try not to .... offended by what Mary said. I'm sure she didn't really mean it.

g How can we .... visiting the Browns this weekend? I'd rather stay at home!

Grammar

Review of verb patterns

1 Complete conversations 1–6 by putting the verb in brackets in the correct form.

1 A: One of my colleagues wanted me .... (buy) a mobile phone like hers.
   B: But yours is quite new. I really object to .... (change) something for the sake of it.

2 A: We could put off .... (make) a decision about installing machinery until next year.
   B: That might mean we need to resort to .... (spend) a huge amount on maintaining the existing machinery.

3 A: Has it always been company policy to avoid .... (give) a refund on sales goods?
   B: Yes. You can issue a credit note but you must insist on .... (see) the receipt.

4 A: I don't recall .... (receive) any notification about the change in dates.
   B: I'm afraid it was a last minute amendment. I do apologise for .... (not/inform) you.

5 A: The Wrights never stop .... (boast) about their children's achievements.
   B: Perhaps you ought to .... (mention) the fact that they have already told you!

6 A: Bill can't stand .... (commute) for three hours every day.
   B: Maybe you should advise him .... (look) for a job closer to home?

2 Complete these sentences using a suitable verb below in the infinitive form with or without *to*.

> strike   complete   feel   provide
> solve   accept   enter

a Several residents heard someone .... the building in the early hours of the morning.
b The management refuse .... responsibility for any damage to property on the premises.
c Under the terms of the contract, we agree .... the work in a period of three weeks.
d The letter was written in such an aggressive tone that it made me .... angry.
e Sam's tutor offered .... him some extra help with his thesis.
f Can anyone help .... this confusion about transportation costs?
g The baggage handlers at the airport threatened .... if their demands were not met.

3 Match the sentence halves using the prepositions below and the correct form of the verb in brackets. Three of the prepositions are <u>not</u> needed.

> at   for   on   of   from   by

a Please don't blame me …
b I can't believe Anne's supervisor actually accused her …
c The police praised everyone …
d Most hotels try to discourage guests …
e Voters will never forgive the government …
f Officials tried to prevent the spectators …
g That scruffy old rucksack reminds me …

1 (smoke) in their bedrooms.
2 (forget) what you should have remembered yourself.
3 (not/live) up to their election promises.
4 (steal) her own office stationery.
5 (rush) onto the pitch at the end of the game.
6 (travel) across Europe when I was a student.
7 (not/panic) during the bomb scare.

Listening Part 4 Multiple matching

1 Read the instructions and questions for 2 which are about people discussing friendship. Which statements reflect your own opinions or experiences?

2 🎧 Listen to five short extracts and complete the exam task.

For 1–5, choose from A–H the people's attitudes towards friendships.

A The only people I feel I can make demands on are my friends.

B I think I can honestly say that I have never really had a best friend.

C I expect my friends to place our friendship above everything.

D We often give friends a one-sided impression of our true selves.

E Friends are people you can invite to a dinner party at the last minute.

F I always take advantage of opportunities to meet people.

G My friendships mean far more to me than even my job.

H I socialise with people of a similar background to myself.

Speaker 1 ☐ 1

Speaker 2 ☐ 2

Speaker 3 ☐ 3

Speaker 4 ☐ 4

Speaker 5 ☐ 5

For 6–10, choose from A–H what upsets people about friendships.

A not being able to rely on friends in times of trouble

B being bothered by someone who won't accept the friendship is over

C constantly being forced to make new friends

D realising that your friendship is no longer of any value

E dealing with friends' emotional problems

F losing touch with people who have been your friends since childhood

G being let down by friends at work

H knowing their position in the group is what matters to your friends

Speaker 1 ☐ 6

Speaker 2 ☐ 7

Speaker 3 ☐ 8

Speaker 4 ☐ 9

Speaker 5 ☐ 10

English in Use   Part 3 Error correction

1 Read the article below about interviews, ignoring any mistakes. How does the writer advise people to perfect their interview technique?

a in front of a mirror
b with someone they know well
c with an expert in the field

2 Read the text again. There is either a spelling or a punctuation error in most lines. Write the correctly spelt word or show the correct punctuation. Indicate the lines which are correct with a tick (✓).

Examples
  0   ✓
 00 *answers*
000 *receive*

Preparing for your first interview

  0   Before going to an interview, you should go through a mock interview.

 00 This will give the opportunity to try out your technique and answers' live.

000 It is also a chance to recieve constructive feedback from someone who can

01 guide you, towards improving your interview style and presentation.

02 Just one mock interview will result in a noticable improvement in your

03 interview skills. Why? For the same reason that a speech is not a speech

04 while it is still on paper or floating in your head. It s only a speech when you

05 give it verbaly. The first time you give it in front of an audience, it will come out

06 nothing like the one you prepared. It is the same with being interviewed. It is not

07 enough to look at a question and say, 'Yeah, I know the answer to that one'

08 you must practise your answer live and in front of someone else. This is not

09 the time to talk to yourself in front of a mirror. Seek out a proffessional and

10 have the session videotaped. Then you will have two opinions – the interviewers

11 and your own. Remember that you get a totally different affect when listening

12 to yourself from when you are watching yourself saying something. Just as your

13 voice always sounds different on tape, so do your answers. 'Did I really say that?'

14 you'll ask. You will be glad the image is captured on tape and not in a potential

15 employer's mind. For maximum effectivness, review your answers and go through

16 a second mock interview. This will give you confidence in your first interview.

Customs and traditions

Reading Part 2 Gapped text

1 Read the text and paragraphs A–G quickly and find out:
a who the Sami are.
b what annual custom the writer takes part in.
c if the writer enjoyed the experience.

2 Read the whole text again and match paragraphs A–G with gaps 1–6. There is one extra paragraph.

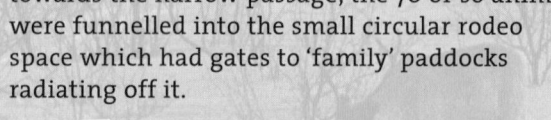

I wanted to spend a few days brooding under the midday moon. A heated log cabin and maybe a sauna, in Sweden's far north, above the Arctic circle. And I would meditate on the loss of light and the
5 loneliness, in a drawn-out, snowy, winter world where the sun never shines. And that's what I said when the editor asked what I'd like to write about and I was quickly packed off to Övre Soppero with photographer Mark. 'Oh, it's never dark up here,'
10 our host Per-Nils Päiviö insisted when we met him and his wife, Britt-Marie, who was preparing a reindeer stew with lingonberry sauce.

The next two days and nights in the warmth of the cabin and the traditional circular hut covered in
15 turf, with wood-burning stoves – and yes, a sauna – were cosy enough. Informative, too, as – along with a breakfast of pancakes – I was given a thorough education in the ancient and barely altered life of the reindeer-herding Sami people of northern
20 Sweden. Just as I was beginning to relax, I found myself being introduced to 'my' reindeer. I was handed the reins along with some sparse instructions: pull left for faster, right for stop.

Tonight Pers-Nils was taking us by snowmobile to
25 the huts by the network of corrals where the families lived over the three-day round-up. But he, Mark and I were spending the night in a lavvu, guarding the reindeer. Back home I had discovered that 'lavvu', which had appeared on
30 my itinerary, meant a tent. I imagined a nice, warm tourist tent. Now, 'spending the night' began to ring alarm bells.

3 ☐

Somehow, I survived, stiff and a little mad with lack of sleep. Then the round-up began. All the
35 families revved up their snowmobiles and spread out in a mysterious pattern, surrounding the reindeer. Dogs barked, people shouted to each other in the grey light, and 7,000 reindeer ran in the desired direction: into a large corral. They
40 were herded by a long line of people on foot towards the narrow passage; the 70 or so animals were funnelled into the small circular rodeo space which had gates to 'family' paddocks radiating off it.

A
But for me, the best thing was that it had the Hotel
Ralleran, an old, wooden building devotedly restored,
75 and a shrine to simplicity and comfort. It had
beautiful, pale-timbered walls, wooden floors, light,
space and the most comfortable bed I have ever
slept in and at last a jacuzzi.

B
I sat in the family paddock by a fire of seven-foot logs
80 and choked on woodsmoke. 'Ah', a fur-encased elderly
lady laughed. 'The smoke follows you. It means that
you will be rich.' Or so her daughter translated. What
she was probably saying was: 'Who is this stranger?'

C
Dinner was delicious and warming, and marked our
85 introduction to Swedish Lapland as guests of the
Sami, the indigenous people who were here long
before the Swedes, Norwegians, Finns and Russians
arrived. 'Snow. Northern lights. The moon for two
weeks every month. You can go out in the forest in
90 the middle of December and you hardly need a torch',
he commented. Despite my initial reservation, I was
becoming intrigued by this dark world and was
actually keen to start our 'adventure'.

D
Yet they showed a demonstrable desire to keep their
95 Sami heritage, not as a museum exhibit but an actual
existence. It's one reason why the Sami are inviting
small groups of visitors to share something of their
traditions and so they can try to sustain their
reindeer-herding way of life.

E
100 My fears turned out to be justified. The Sami version
of a tepee had a layer of reindeer skins over the bare,
snow-covered, and where I was sleeping, lumpy earth.
The fifteen-centimetre gap around the bottom was
apparently to let the fresh air in. I spent most of the
105 time perched on my elbows, staring at the embers of
the fire in the centre.

F
The reindeer took over immediately, either sauntering
along or racing his best mate. My performance did
lose the respect of the other guides, but thankfully
110 they were kind about it and excitedly started talking
about tomorrow's agenda. They had brought together
the 7,000 reindeer of the whole district, and
tomorrow we would be able to participate in the
great annual separation of the herds into family
115 groups. This is done according to the signs on the ears
of each yearling calf and to allocate the winter
grazing. Spending a day with 7,000 reindeer –
naturally, I was thrilled!

G
My job was to stand to one side and head off the
120 stragglers and escapees. This is done by flapping the
arms up and down (a good way of keeping warm) and
hooting. Even the most desultory of flaps will
persuade a wayward reindeer – as I discovered to my
relief – to get back into the crowd.

45 I declined to wrestle with a reindeer, but Mark
put down his camera and became a veritable
Sami by grabbing it and shouting, 'It's one of
ours', as he was dragged across the corral floor.
Having no interest in honour, I begged for a bed
50 with walls around it that night, and maybe even
with a jacuzzi.

We had another magical, frozen ride back on the
snowmobile and then a car to Kiruna, the town
that contains the Sami parliament and is home
55 to the Swedish iron ore mine. The mine has
contracted and has utterly changed the
traditional herding land, and is part of what
threatens the Sami way of life.

5 ☐

After a day off, I visited some Sami pupils at a
60 local school. They take some of their lessons in
their own language and learn about skills and
traditions that are rapidly being forgotten. All the
youngsters were looking to the future and making
plans for their lives beyond reindeer herding.

6 ☐

65 Even the likes of me can recognise how
privileged I was to participate in that. And we
were told that the extra hands can even be
useful: Mark apparently was an asset, not just a
gawking outsider. Me? Well, now I've warmed up
70 a bit, I am very grateful to have had such an
extraordinary experience. All I can hope is that I
didn't make life too difficult for my patient hosts.

Vocabulary

Words with similar meanings (1)

1 Match the words in 1–5 with definitions a or b.

1 imaginary / imaginative
   a good at thinking up new ideas
   b existing only in the imagination

2 exhausting / exhaustive
   a extremely tiring
   b thorough and detailed

3 conscience / conscientious
   a doing something thoroughly and carefully
   b a feeling for what is morally right

4 satisfying / satisfactory
   a giving a feeling of pleasure
   b sufficiently good or suitable

5 sensible / sensitive
   a realistic and practical
   b aware of others' feelings

2 Use words from 1 to complete these sentences.

a Work attained in all classes has been .... in terms of the school's standards this year.

b Samson is a very .... writer and always constructs an intricate and fascinating plot.

c The government's survey into unemployment is the most .... document of its kind.

d I can't believe Chris cheated in the exam! Doesn't he have a .... ?

e Our school is .... to problems facing new students and we aim to support them fully.

Compound nouns

3 Circle the one word on the right which <u>cannot</u> be combined with a–e to form a compound noun.

a hand   book/shake/bar/basin
b film   crew/goer/picture/script
c news   agent/flash/data/reader
d side   effect/mark/track/street
e work   hour/shop/place/out

4 Make compound nouns by matching a–e with 1–5.

a take   1 through
b turn   2 over
c set   3 out
d hand   4 back
e break   5 down

5 Use the nouns you formed in 4 to complete these sentences.

a The surprisingly low .... at the tennis tournament was due to torrential rain.

b An unsuccessful .... bid was made by an unknown investor last year.

c Research into hereditary illness has resulted in a welcome .... for scientists.

d A .... will be distributed to all students at the end of the lecture.

e Unfortunately, there has been a temporary .... in the peace negotiations.

f It is reputed that the oil company has an annual .... of forty million dollars.

g The .... of power to the newly elected government took place yesterday.

h There has been a .... at the prison – three inmates are thought to have escaped.

Grammar

Gerunds and infinitives

1 Complete gaps 1–8 with the correct form of the verbs below. You may need to add a preposition.

■ be   waste   establish   cope   send
travel   go   expand

Tim wasn't looking forward 1 .... on his first business trip to Latvia in the middle of winter. He wasn't very keen 2 .... in icy conditions and he'd never been very good at 3 .... with cold temperatures. In any case, he didn't believe 4 .... time making personal visits when a phone call or email would do just as well. He objected 5 .... told what to do, but his boss had insisted 6 .... him there for a brief meeting. The company had been thinking 7 .... into that part of the world for some time and had already succeeded 8 .... contacts in Central and Eastern Europe.

Winter in Latvia

2 Match sentence halves a–f with 1–6 and put the verbs in brackets in the correct form.

a   Did Sally actually manage …
b   Is it true that Sam threatened …
c   What do you hope …
d   I don't think we should risk …
e   Would you prefer …
f   The accused man denied …

1   (do) in ten years' time?
2   (convince) Andrea to watch that horror film?
3   (drive) to the airport in case there's a traffic jam.
4   (have) a vegetarian dish for your main course?
5   (resign) if he wasn't given a salary increase?
6   (steal) the money but no one believed him.

Relative clauses

3 Combine the sentences in a–g using a relative pronoun and, where necessary, a preposition.

a   This is the old car. William used it to travel all over Europe.
b   The new train can reach speeds of 300 km per hour. The train's design is certainly innovative.
c   The Welsh mountains are very beautiful. I spent most of my childhood there.
d   We met other employees. Most had been with the company for a few years.
e   Winning the World Cup was one of those wonderful moments. You feel perfectly happy.
f   The film star is the subject of much gossip. She will be at the premiere in New York tomorrow.
g   The accident happened. We cannot explain it.

Listening

Part 1 Note taking

1 Read the exam task in 2 below. What do you already know about Mount Uluru (Ayers Rock) and what it means to the Aboriginal people?

2 🎧 Listen to a guide talking to a group of tourists about to visit Mount Uluru in Australia, and complete the notes.

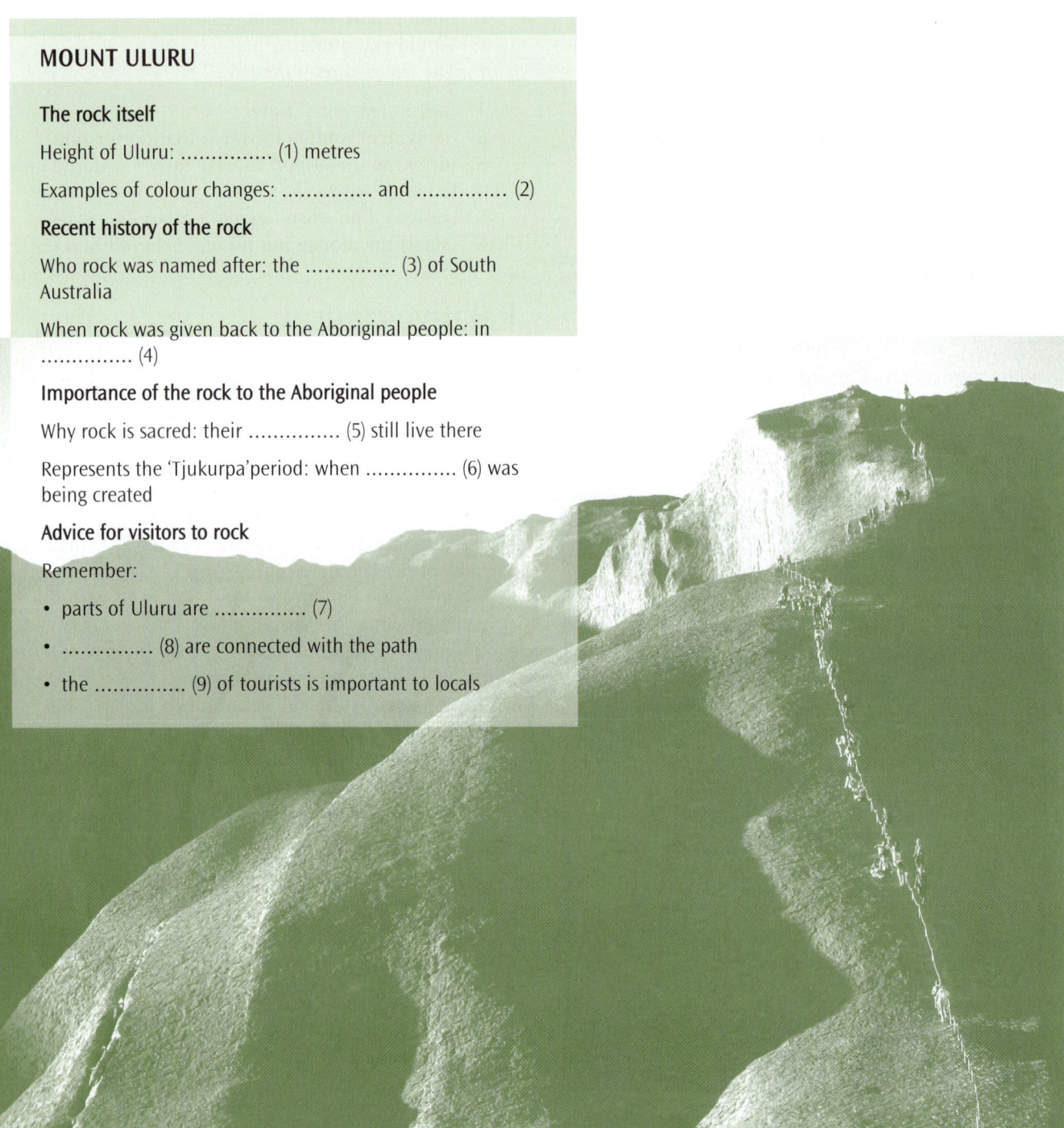

MOUNT ULURU

The rock itself

Height of Uluru: .... (1) metres

Examples of colour changes: .... and .... (2)

Recent history of the rock

Who rock was named after: the .... (3) of South Australia

When rock was given back to the Aboriginal people: in .... (4)

Importance of the rock to the Aboriginal people

Why rock is sacred: their .... (5) still live there

Represents the 'Tjukurpa' period: when .... (6) was being created

Advice for visitors to rock

Remember:

• parts of Uluru are .... (7)

• .... (8) are connected with the path

• the .... (9) of tourists is important to locals

English in Use

Part 6 Gapped text

1 Read the text opposite about a Japanese festival, ignoring the gaps, and find out how the festival started.

2 Read the text again and fill gaps 1–6 using six of clauses A–J. There are three extra phrases.

A which was megalithic in its proportions
B which is usually lit up at night with coloured lights
C which belong in the school playground
D which are hammered into place around the scaffolding
E which transforms itself into a winter dream world
F which bears no resemblance to a backyard snowman
G which had extremely humble origins
H which is not an easy thing to do
I which freezes them into hard-as-rock mortar
J *which is the coldest time of the year in Japan*

STATUES OF SAPPORO

Every year at the beginning of February, (0) ......J........ Sapporo, the capital of Japan's northernmost island, attracts a cavalcade of visitors. They come to marvel at the city, (1) .... , heaving with glittering monsters and ice-maidens, palaces and pyramids. More than 2,000,000 people take to the streets, waiting for the frosted statues to appear.

The festival, (2) .... , is today a high-profile international event. It began in 1950, when a couple of high school students fashioned six snow statues in Odori Park; five years later, members of Sapporo's Defence Force sowed the seeds of the now world-famous festival by building the first statue (3) .... Snow sculpting might sound like one of those skills (4) .... , but it actually takes a lot of patience and artistic talent to form these snow giants. First, a wooden structure is built. Large blocks of snow are then cut from the ground. The blocks, (5) .... , are then hosed down with water, (6) .... It is only then that the painstaking job of sculpting the masterpiece begins.

The combined result of all this carving and sculpting is a crystal-like dreamscape of frosted versions of many famous buildings, including the Statue of Liberty, the Great Wall of China, and the Leaning Tower of Pisa.

Looking ahead

Reading

Parts 1 and 4 Multiple matching

1 Read the article opposite about Mars and answer the questions below.

   a   What is 'terraforming'?
   b   What was exciting about the discovery made by 'Spirit' and 'Opportunity'?
   c   What are some of the problems the project could face?

2 Read the article again and write in which section (A–F) each of 1–12 below is mentioned.

recent optimism about a scientific breakthrough	1 …
features that Mars previously had but which no longer exist	2 … 3 …
the cost and time involved in putting terraforming into practice	4 …
a potential solution to the problem of Earth's growing population	5 …
vital actions that would help to launch terraforming	6 …
evidence that may prove the existence of life on Mars	7 …
an important formal discussion of an innovative idea	8 …
dismay at human's potential for destruction	9 … 10 …
a construction to change Mars despite not actually being on the planet	11 …
the possibility of similar origins for life forms on Earth and Mars	12 …

LIFE ON MARS?

A Billions of years after the last seas and rivers dried up on Mars, scientists believe they may be able to restore the Red Planet to its former glory – by turning it into a blue world with streams, green fields and fresh breezes, and
5 filling it with Earthly creatures. Ultimately, this new Earthly paradise could even provide mankind's increasing numbers with a new home. This revolutionary scheme of 'terraforming' recently formed the focus of a major international debate hosted by America's space agency,
10 NASA. Leading researchers as well as science-fiction writers, including Arthur C. Clarke, were included in the guest list.

B Terraforming has always been considered the stuff of fiction, according to NASA astrobiologist Michael Meyer.
15 But now, with a multi-billion dollar Mars research programme drawn up by NASA, there is the chance to ask what the real possibilities are of transforming Mars, and to explore the potential effects. If the project were found to be feasible, it would take decades to achieve
20 and would require massive expenditure. Foremost among the critics is Paul Murdin of the Institute of Astronomy, Cambridge. He believes the idea of terraforming Mars is extreme but not ridiculous and that, he believes, is the worst thing about it. 'If it was just a silly science-fiction
25 idea', he says, 'one could laugh it off, but the idea is actually a real one. I find it incredible that mankind is mucking up this world at an amazing pace and, at the same time, talking about doing the same to another planet.'

C 30 While the debate rages over the rights and wrongs of the project, the investigation of Mars continues. Over past months, astronomers have become increasingly confident that they will find Martian life forms after decades of disappointment. Two robot rovers, 'Spirit' and
35 'Opportunity', which are both investigating the planet at the moment, have detected strong evidence that water, mixed with soil, exists in large amounts. Excitement over this discovery was heightened recently when two different groups of scientists revealed they had found traces of
40 methane in the Martian atmosphere. This gas is a waste product of living creatures and could have come from Martian microbes living in the Red Planet's soil.

D It is the risk that terraforming poses to these organisms that outrages scientists, such as Dr Lisa Pratt, a NASA
45 astrobiologist. She finds it very depressing that, before it has even been discovered that there is life on Mars, people are talking about projects that would wipe out all these strange life forms. As she sees it, the whole thing is ethically wrong. While she is not the only protester,

50 scientists have already started exploring the problems they would face if the project went ahead. Engineers would have to find a way to thicken the planet's atmosphere, and to heat it up. (At present its surface temperature can plunge to minus 60°C and below.) Both
55 goals could be achieved at the same time, according to researchers. One idea is to build a large mirror, many miles in diameter, and place it in orbit above Mars. This would focus the Sun's rays onto a polar icecap, melting it and releasing its frozen carbon dioxide. The carbon
60 dioxide would then trigger greenhouse heating.

E Alternatively, scientists could construct industrial plants which would generate super-greenhouse gases. These gases are thousands of times more effective than carbon dioxide at trapping heat. The plants would be built at
65 strategic sites across the planet and would set off global temperature rises. Thickening the Martian atmosphere would also protect its surface from the ultra-violet radiation on its surface and which would otherwise kill most Earth-like life forms on the planet. According to Dr
70 Chris McKay – based at NASA's research centre in California, these methods could provide the terraforming project with a crucial kick-start. With a thicker and warmer atmosphere, ice trapped in the Martian soil would melt and could be used to sustain agriculture.
75 With plants and trees imported from Earth growing and producing oxygen, the atmosphere would become slowly more Earth-like. We should, he urges, get serious about sending life to Mars.

F But other scientists are more cautious. Monica Grady, a
80 planetary scientist at the Natural History Museum, London, points out that Mars used to have an atmosphere, but it disappeared for reasons that are still unclear. If scientists restore Mars's atmosphere, she claims, it could just disappear again. Devastating things
85 would have been done to the planet for a temporary effect and that would certainly not be ethical. These concerns are shared by Pratt, who believes the philosophical implications of finding life on Mars would be profound. If Martian life is found to have a different
90 genetic code to ours, then living beings must have evolved separately on two neighbouring worlds, she says. And this implies that life could be found throughout the galaxy. If, however, Martian and Earthly life turn out to have the same genetic code, that will suggest that one planet was
95 contaminated by the other – probably as a result of meteorite impacts. If that is the case, we may all be Martian in origin, so for us, terraforming will mean returning to our roots.

Vocabulary

Two-part phrasal verbs

1 Write nouns for phrasal verbs a–d and match them with meanings 1–5 below.

Example

burst out   *outburst 3*

a cut back   ....
b fall down   ....
c bring up   ....
d put in   ....

1 failure of something or someone
2 raising a child
3 ~~a passing moment of anger~~
4 reduction in the amount of something
5 effort given to a project, etc.

2 Circle the correct particle to complete sentences a–f, then match them with meanings 1–6.

a The armed robber told the cashier to hand *in/on/over* the money in the till.
b What do you make *of/up/to* this letter from my ex-boyfriend? I'm not sure how to interpret it.
c Our elderly neighbour passed *off/away/up* last week so the family are selling his house.
d The manager is unable to speak at the conference tomorrow so I'm going to stand *in/up/to* for him and talk to the delegates.
e I was prepared to lend my brother some money but he turned *back/over/down* my offer.
f Two people were knocked *away/off/down* by a car on a pedestrian crossing this morning.

1 take someone's place
2 give (not voluntarily)
3 hit and cause to fall
4 die
5 reject
6 understand by

3 Match the two-part phrasal verbs a–f with meanings 1–6.

a hand out   1 understand
b make out   2 distribute
c knock out   3 lose consciousness
d stand out   4 produce or make
e turn out   5 be noticeable
f pass out   6 eliminate in a competition

4 Use the correct form of the phrasal verbs from 3 to complete these sentences.

a .... leaflets in the High Street has to be one of the most boring jobs!
b There's no doubt that wearing designer clothes makes you .... in a crowd.
c How can Tim be a medical student when he .... as soon as he sees blood?
d Nobody can .... what her motives were in telling so many lies.
e Unfortunately the basketball team got .... in the first round of the tournament.
f This factory is our most productive – it .... an amazing 1,000 cars a week.

Grammar Future forms

1 Read the text about an unusual play and use the correct future form of the verbs below to complete gaps 1–8.

> sell out   know   find out   talk   meet
> perform   not effect   give

Mike Leigh is a playwright who works without a script, so the actors have to improvise. For this reason, his new play does not even have a title. But by next Friday morning, Leigh 1 .... out whether his new play 2 .... with the approval of the critics or not. On Thursday evening, the cast 3 .... 'A New Play by Mike Leigh' for the first time and before an audience who 4 .... virtually nothing about it.

The fact that this is his first play for 12 years is unlikely to be a problem and 5 .... its performance at the box office. Theatregoers expect that tickets for the play's first run of performances 6 .... long before the first night, when it is hoped the play 7 .... a title. One thing, however, is certain – whatever the play is about, Leigh fans 8 .... about it for many weeks to come.

2 Which of the expressions in a–f is followed by
1   the infinitive with *to*
2   *of + ing*?

a   just about?
b   bound
c   on the point
d   certain
e   no possibility whatsoever
f   no chance

3 Use some of the expressions in 2 to describe your plans for the year ahead – starting from now!

Grammar Extra

Adjective and adverb order

4 The categories below show adjective order before a noun. Put the adjectives into the correct place.

> china   orange   Russian   young   rectangular
> ancient   oval   purple   Chinese   silk
> fascinating   tiny   disgusting   heavy

your opinion	....
size/weight	....
age	....
shape	....
colour	....
country of origin	....
material	....

5 Answer questions a–d about adverbs.

a   What is the correct order for the adverbial phrases of place and manner in this sentence?
The Prime Minister spoke.
(at the conference/very well)
Where could you add *on Saturday*?

b   Where would you normally put the adverb *probably* in these sentences?
Christopher knows the way to our house.
Jill doesn't know the way.

c   Which emphasising adverb would you use in these sentences?
I quite/just agree with you.
I quite/just love your new flat.

d   Where would you put the adverbs *very* or *pretty* in this sentence?
I can see the ship clearly on the horizon now.

Listening Part 3 Multiple choice

1 Look at the photos of Sally and Pete Fletcher planning a trip across Siberia on motorbikes. What difficulties do you think they may face?

2 🎧 Listen to an interview with the couple, and choose the best answers for 1–6.

1 Pete says their forthcoming trip will challenge them because of the
   A kind of terrain they are crossing.
   B enormous distances they are covering.
   C means of transport they are using.
   D length of time they are taking.

2 Sally says she and Pete were motivated to go on the trip because of a
   A need for excitement.
   B lifelong ambition.
   C desire to earn money.
   D plan to write a book.

3 How does Pete feel about tackling the journey?
   A He thinks that their chances of succeeding are above average.
   B He would prefer not to talk about what might happen.
   C He's excited about the dangers they're about to experience.
   D He suspects they're about to face their toughest challenge yet.

4 According to Sally, how have friends and family reacted to their journey?
   A They have offered them their help if it should be needed.
   B They have expressed their doubts about the success of the venture.
   C They have advised them which route to take across Siberia.
   D They have encouraged them to carry on and not be dispirited.

5 They are going to ensure their safety and well-being during the journey by
   A carrying enough supplies for the whole trip.
   B avoiding routes which are known to be dangerous.
   C making sure they have enough hot meals.
   D wearing suitable clothing for the climate.

6 What comment does Sally make about the weather during their journey?
   A Unexpected bad weather often interferes with timings for stops.
   B Whatever the weather, they will try to stick to the scheduled stop times.
   C If the weather is against them, they will be forced to abandon their trip.
   D Bad weather has less effect on motorbikes than other forms of transport.

English in Use Part 1 Multiple-choice cloze

1 Read the text below, ignoring the gaps, to find out why the 'body clock' is important.

2 Read the text again and complete gaps 1–15 with the best option (A, B, C or D).

Example
0 B

A FUTURE IN THE DARK

For many of us, we are working, travelling and shopping in hours that used to be (0) ..*B*... for relaxation and sleep. But, according to the results of tests being (1)............... by scientists, we are no longer getting enough darkness in our lives. In fact, (2)............... shows that a growing number of health and environmental problems are (3)............... a loss of darkness. This has (4)............... one expert to predict that things can only get worse as we become a 24/7 world.

Life has evolved with a day/night cycle. People who go (5)............... this day/night rhythm will notice an adverse impact on their immune systems, and that's not a good (6)............... . We are (7)............... a conflict between what our mind wants, and what our internal body clock (8)............... us for. Some experts (9)............... that our biological clock is similar to the conductor of an orchestra, with the multiple rhythms of the body (10)............... the various orchestra sections.

The body clock is (11)............... on the light/dark cycle and it governs us for every (12)............... of activity and rest in our lives. It ensures that all our various internal systems are working together – this is its sole (13)............... . By moving to 24-hour living, and not taking into (14)............... the dark side, we will effectively be throwing away the advantages of evolution, (15)............... we care to admit it or not.

0	A conserved	B reserved	C upheld	D defended
1	A carried out	B carried through	C worked up	D worked off
2	A demonstration	B display	C research	D confirmation
3	A prone to	B open to	C due to	D next to
4	A pronounced	B prompted	C projected	D prodded
5	A down with	B without	C through	D behind
6	A notice	B indicator	C sign	D figure
7	A creating	B contributing	C giving	D increasing
8	A arranges	B prepares	C orders	D disposes
9	A explain	B discuss	C enquire	D debate
10	A describing	B corresponding	C expressing	D representing
11	A done	B based	C decided	D established
12	A prospect	B attitude	C position	D type
13	A reason	B project	C purpose	D desire
14	A interest	B importance	C detail	D account
15	A so that	B whether	C unless	D in case

Review Units 1–3

1 Correct the mistakes in adjective and adverb order.

a Tim had a rather small extremely fascinating group of friends.
b Did you at the beach enjoy yourself yesterday?
c You don't have to make immediately a decision.
d We found the pretty restaurant easily.
e What a table disgusting oval wooden old!
f Ted doesn't probably want to come to the party.
g I love just your new dress.
h What a rectangular dirty enormous pencil case!
i Brenda likes quite being on her own.

2 Read definitions a–g, then write the compound nouns.

a a place where things are made or repaired
   = work...............
b a problem which makes a situation worse
   = set...............
c an important development in a situation
   = break...............
d someone who sells papers and magazines
   = news...............
e the written text of a movie
   = film...............
f an unexpected result of a situation or action
   = side...............
g the number of people attending an event
   = turn...............

3 Add suitable verbs to sentences a–e to make two-part phrasal verbs.

a What makes Jim .... out in a crowd is his long, blond hair.
b I don't know what to .... of this strange phone message on the answering machine.
c Unfortunately, our request for a loan to finance the deal was .... down by the bank.
d This year the team is determined not to get .... out in the first round.
e Sally .... out after the accident and has no recollection of what happened.

4 Put the words in the correct order beginning with the words in bold.

Example

a *the photograph John I showed the.*
   I showed John the photograph.
b her for bicycle brother a bought birthday **Susie** his.
c me a fortune **My** new car cost!
d seeing Robert's insisted **The authorities** visa on.
e late for tonight me because **Save** I'll be some supper.
f coffee the **Fetch** you would visitors some?
g extra the holiday students an promised day's **The** principal.
h having wisdom **My** dentist recommended teeth taken out two.
i it to careful leave appliance the switched not on after **Be** using.

5 Complete the adjectives in sentences a–e.

a Good teachers are sens............... to the needs of their students.
b After an exhaust............... international trip, the President will take a break at his summer residence.
c Children love stories and imagin............... heroes.
d One of the most satisf............... things about sport is that it helps people develop team skills.
e Fortunately, all our members of staff are all consci............... and hard-working.

6 Correct the mistakes with gerunds and infinitives in sentences a–g.

a We recommend to wash the appliance before using it.
b Bob would rather to work for himself than for someone else.
c Keri's parents insisted of her learning how to drive.
d When did Paul and Sally stop to go out with each other?
e Anyone fancy to go to the cinema tonight?
f The football team succeeded on winning the European Cup.
g We would prefer the witness telling the court in his own words exactly what happened.

7 Complete sentences a–e using one of the nouns below.

■ upbringing cutbacks downfall input outburst

a As a member of the student union, we would very much like your .... on this matter.

b She is normally a very calm, relaxed person. I don't know where that sudden .... came from.

c The scandal surrounding last year's festival brought about its ....

d I regret to say that due to the .... , we will be unable to have our annual party this year.

e What do you think has the greatest influence on your life, your .... or your school education?

8 Complete sentences a–e using a suitable expression with *get*.

a These endless discussions are getting us .... It's time we reached an agreement.

b You should meet my sister. You'd get .... really well with her.

c Let's get .... to business. What's the first item on the agenda?

d As it's getting .... for 7 o'clock, I think we should draw the session to a close.

e We can't get .... of going to the party without offending someone.

9 Complete a–f with a relative pronoun and, where necessary, a preposition. More than one answer may be possible.

a This is the place .... the accident occurred.

b Africa, ... culture is extremely diverse, is a huge continent.

c The poet, ... very little is known, lived in the north of Scotland.

d It would be interesting to know .... Thomas decided to leave the football club.

e There was a time .... deer roamed wild through these woods.

f Debbie has painted numerous landscapes, some .... are on display in the exhibition.

10 Choose the best adjective to complete sentences 1–5.

1 The teaching staff were .... in their intention to improve examination results.
   a depressed   b resolute   c curious

2 Despite the disappointing sales figures, we are .... about the future of the company.
   a realistic   b curious   c optimistic

3 I now feel .... that I can make myself understood when I'm speaking Italian.
   a cheerful   b depressed   c confident

4 It is hardly .... to expect to fulfil all our dreams and ambitions in life.
   a realistic   b pessimistic   c optimistic

5 Everyone is .... with Sarah's moody behaviour.
   a fed up   b depressed   c pessimistic

11 Use future forms to write sentences about the likelihood of the following happening.

Example
the world's population increasing
The population of the world is bound to increase, because …

a humans living on Mars

....

b the cost of public transport rising

....

c robots becoming part of our daily life

....

d all the countries of the world speaking the same language

....

e your country's football team winning the world cup

....

f your class passing the exam

....

Into the wild

Reading Part 2 Gapped text

1 Read the article, and paragraphs A–G, about learning to dive, and find out what words a–c refer to.

a double-decker bus   b swimming pool   c 'buddy'

2 Read the article again and match paragraphs A–G with gaps 1–6. Remember there is one extra paragraph.

I was on holiday in the Dominican Republic with my friend when our hotel offered us a trial scuba dive. You could just put on the equipment in the swimming pool and try it for a while. My friend wasn't remotely
5 interested in getting her hair wet, let along going scuba-diving, but it was something I'd always liked the idea of, so I gave it a go.

1 ....

Each piece looked intimidating as I put it on and I was alarmed at suddenly being in charge of the one thing
10 we can't survive without – the air we breathe. But in reality, it's no different from driving a car. You have an air gauge for your tank, which you watch as if it were the fuel supply, and a depth gauge that's like reading the speedometer. After a while, everything becomes
15 second nature.

2 ....

Suddenly, I'd discovered this completely silent world. I've been a make-up artist since I left school at 18; it's an industry where everyone is always chatting. Although there were people around during the dive,
20 the experience was entirely my own as you can't talk. I'd wanted to try a calming therapy like yoga or meditation for ages, but never got anywhere because I was always distracted by something. Here, I had to keep my breathing steady and before I knew it, I was
25 completely relaxed, lost in these beautiful colours and a myriad of sea creatures.

3 ....

I knew then that I really wanted to take up this new hobby seriously. So when I flew back to England I started an Introduction to Diving Skills course at a
30 nearby swimming pool three days later. Going from the Dominican Republic to my local pool fortunately wasn't actually as bad as I'd expected.

4 ....

I knew that your emergency air supply is actually with your dive partner, how the thing you absolutely must
35 not do is to hold your breath, because you risk bursting a lung.

And you should also swot up on where you want to go diving. For example, I really enjoyed history when I was at school, so I love wreck-diving to see it all come to life
40 and observe what I've been reading about. Diving lets you see things, in their natural surroundings, which no one has seen before.

5 ....

Our breaks away triggered my decision to teach scuba-diving. And having done the introduction course, I
45 realised how important it was to learn slowly and thoroughly – on holiday I saw people in the water who really shouldn't have been there. They didn't have a clue about the dangers of coming up too quickly, of being too long underwater, or of not watching their air.
50 I thought it would be good to learn more, to become a better diver myself and to help others dive safely.

6 ....

I teach once a month now at one of the top dive centres in the UK. It's so rewarding, especially when you come up with someone who has done their first
55 dive – they've discovered an exciting new world without boundaries – a world I love so much.

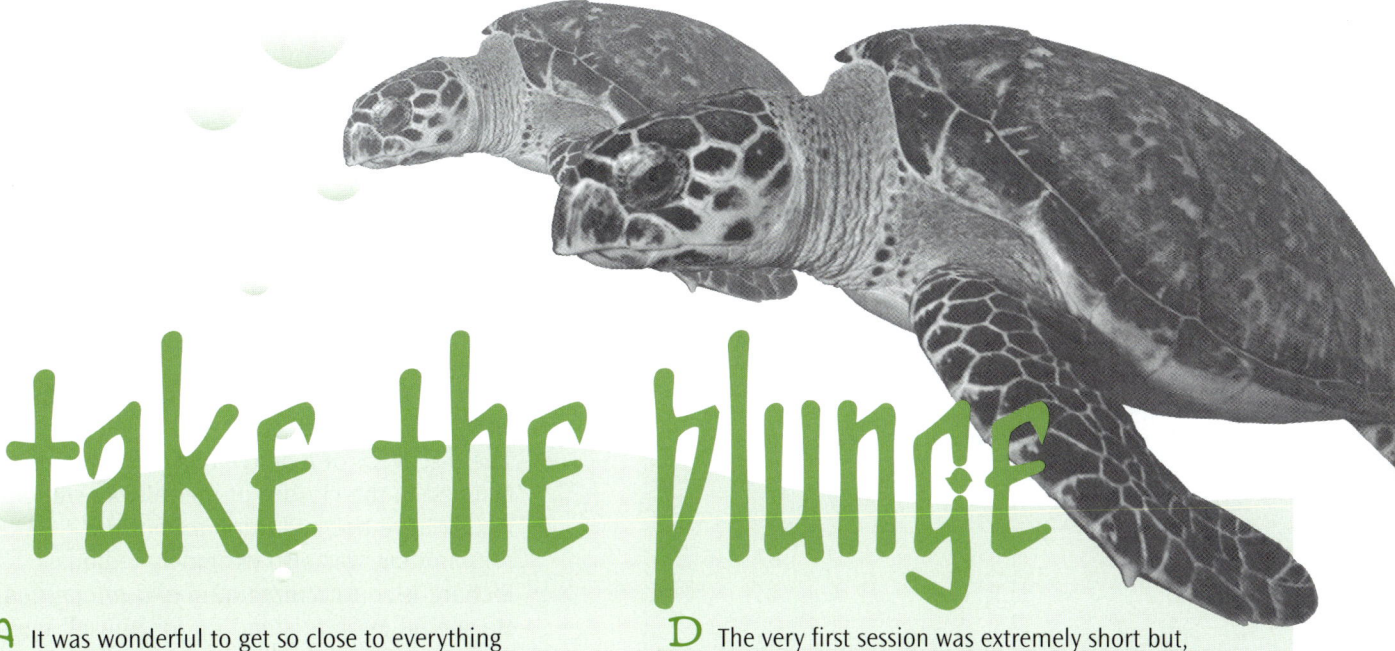

take the plunge

A It was wonderful to get so close to everything below the surface of the sea, and to spend as long as I liked just observing and moving along completely
60 weightless. It felt so effortless. I saw a turtle on that first dive, not a giant one, but at a metre from head to tail, it was big enough for me. It left me completely in awe, even though it totally ignored me.

B To become a competent diver, he recommended
65 the following steps. First, take an introductory course, which consists of five swimming pool lessons. Next, do the five theory modules, which end with a multiple-choice test. But he also pointed out that to qualify to dive with a 'buddy' of the same qualification or higher,
70 you need to complete a further four supervised dives, this time in open water.

C As well as opening up this forgotten world, it brought me into contact with my partner, Roger. I met him whilst on a training excursion – part of the course
75 – to Crystal Waters, where they've deliberately sunk a double-decker bus. I'd found the bus but wanted to go back and have another look. My friend had an ear problem so Roger, who'd been standing near us, offered to partner me. We went on countless dives
80 together and now we go on diving holidays together whenever we can.

D The very first session was extremely short but, surprisingly, it was enough time to get to grips with the three sets of equipment. There was a mask and some
85 fins, a regulator (like a snorkel mouthpiece which you breathe through) attached to a tank for the air supply, and a buoyancy control device which you had to inflate or deflate depending on how deep you wanted to dive.

E That first time you go out on your own with
90 someone who's scared and totally dependent on you, it's terrifying for you too. I used to be overly cautious – if they were even slightly worried, I took them straight back to the top. But I've learned that there are a lot of ways to help people relax underwater.

95 F That 20-minute session was followed by a dive in the sea. After that, I was hooked for good. Other than being shown how to put everything on, there was no further training; not something I'd recommend now, but at the time I was blissfully ignorant. I was taken ten
100 metres down and, despite being followed by a guide who monitored my gauges, I had the most wonderful feeling of freedom.

G The real shock came four months later when I did an open water dive at a place called Grangewaters.
105 When I went in, it only had a water temperature of about four degrees. It's full of black mud, so you can't see anything at all. By then I had done all the theory and I had a very thorough grounding in everything that could go wrong.

Vocabulary

Word formation (1)

1 Write adjective forms of these words in the correct column. You may need to change the spelling.

> malice   control   force   argument   memory
> outrage   possibility   inform   submission
> mystery   suspicion   terror   advantage

ive	ious	eous	able	ible

2 Use adjectives from 1 to replace the words in italics in sentences a–i.

a   After the game, the police struggled to deal with the *scandalous* behaviour of the football supporters.

b   Bella's a great friend but she does tend to be *quarrelsome* at times.

c   The discovery of a *dangerous-looking* package resulted in the closure of the railway station.

d   It may have been *educational* but the presentation was also extremely tedious!

e   Richard is so *uncomplaining and unquestioning*. He should learn to stand up for himself more.

f   Don't listen to a word Janet says – it's all *spiteful* gossip.

g   William's *mystifying* disappearance led to a police search of the area where he lived.

h   I think it would be *extremely useful* to get some work experience to help your job application.

i   What is the most *unforgettable* holiday you've had? For me, it's travelling around New Zealand.

Grammar

Past tenses

1 Complete the leaflet by putting the verbs in brackets into the correct form of the present perfect or the past perfect.

HeLP Save THE ORaNG-UTaN

Did you know that ?

- humans 1 .... (cut) down their habitat for years.

- land which 2 .... (previously/cover) with vegetation was cleared for mining and plantation.

- the orang-utan 3 .... (now/lose) 80% of its natural habitat.

- many 4 .... (kill) by farmers who believed orang-utans 5 .... (become) a pest.

- it 6 .... (recently/become) on the endangered list— only less than 50,000 now exist.

Last year a campaign was set up for people who 7 .... (never/show) active interest in conservation to help save the orang-utan.

Grammar Extra

Articles

2 Underline the correct use of the article in each pair of sentences in 1–7.

1 a Some marketing experience is desirable to run (a, no article) **business** successfully.
  b Our local cinema is back in (the, no article) **business** after its refurbishment.
2 a (The, no article) idle **gossip** can often have unexpected consequences.
  b Polly is (a, no article) **well-known** gossip, so don't tell her anything.

3 a (A, no article) previous **experience** is essential for this job.
  b The book outlines all (the, no article) **experiences** the writer had in Africa.
4 a (An, The) **interest** in the museum's latest exhibition has been tremendous.
  b (An, no article) **interest** is payable on this account but it is so low it is not worth having.
5 a (A, The) **country** is undoubtedly a far healthier place to live than the town.
  b (A, no article) **country** which attracts many foreign visitors is Thailand.
6 a This new restaurant definitely has a touch of (the, no article) **class**.
  b (A, no article) **class** of 35 students is almost impossible to teach effectively.
7 a Due to increased security (a, no article) **people** have to put up with long delays at airports.
  b The President urged (a, the) **people** to turn out in force and vote in the referendum.

3 Complete gaps 1–12 with *a*, *an*, *the* or no article.

Every month we're giving away 1 .... magical holiday. Don't miss this unique opportunity to sample 2 .... luxury of our Transglobe holidays in one of 3 .... world's most sought-after destinations: 4 .... Pacific. Or perhaps you have a secret passion to travel to 5 .... destinations such as Venice, experience 6 .... exciting adventure in 7 .... sports car, or learn to cook 8 .... Eastern delicacies in 9 .... Orient? Just log on to our travel service website and, if you don't win, you can find 10 .... latest destinations and advice on how to plan a trip. At 11 .... end of each holiday, we'll give you 12 .... vouchers to be used towards your next holiday with us.

Listening Part 2 Sentence completion

1 Look at the photos. What athletic abilities do you think these animals have?

2 🎧 You are going to hear part of a radio programme about the athleticism of animals. Listen once and complete sentences 1–9.

ANIMAL ATHLETES

One small ant can lift .... 1 times its own body weight.

Ants have an amazingly large number of .... 2.

It takes the cheetah just .... 3 seconds to cover a distance of 100m.

Cheetahs can reach high speeds, thanks to their enlarged internal organs and their .... 4.

The cheetah, however, has a low .... 5.

The fastest fish in the ocean, the sailfish, gets its name from its .... 6.

Springbok are frequently seen jumping in the .... 7 season.

Archer fish catch .... 8 with a 1.5 metre water jet.

The archer fish carry out their shooting in .... 9.

English in Use Part 2 Open cloze

1 Read the text about whale-watching, ignoring the gaps, and find out where the writer went and for how long.

2 Read the text again and complete each of gaps 1–15 with one suitable word.

Example
0   of

A SUMMER AT SEA

Spending a summer in the company (0) ......**of**...... whales off the coast of Patagonia is a (1) .... in a lifetime opportunity. We were on the boat for twelve hours or more every day and you certainly learn a lot about their behaviour – their interest in (2) .... is just as strong!

All we had to do was move a short distance from the coast, switch (3) .... the engine and wait. If a young one approached the boat, the mother would push him away, but (4) .... it was bigger, she would let it play nearby and even come close (5) .... to touch.

Sometimes we could see whales jumping (6) .... of the water almost everywhere. What I noticed (7) .... that when one jumped, others in the distance (8) .... join in. But on some days, there were (9) .... any whales and that situation could (10) .... on for several days because the whales were simply (11) .... far away to be seen.

After (12) .... while, though, we fell into a pattern: we visited one whale and a baby that we had come (13) .... by chance. At first, she would not let her baby approach. However, with time, little (14) .... little, she allowed him to come right up to the boat. To be rewarded (15) .... such trust at the end of our six weeks was amazing.

Health matters

Reading Part 3 Multiple choice

1 Read the text about human athletic abilities and find out what happened in

a   1954.
b   1968.
c   1991.
d   the 1980s.

2 Read the text again and choose the correct answer (A, B, C or D) to questions 1–6.

1   What initial comment does Dr. Jack Wilmore make?
   A   There will always be limits to what the human body can achieve.
   B   It will become more and more difficult for athletes to break records.
   C   Athletics will become one of the most popular forms of exercise.
   D   Athletes will continue to surprise us with what they can achieve.

2   The writer mentions athletes like Bannister and Beamon in order to
   A   demonstrate the effect their determination to win had on them.
   B   prove that even their amazing achievements can be bettered.
   C   exemplify what athletes can achieve under stressful conditions.
   D   demonstrate how accurately we can measure what athletes are capable of.

3   Dr. Wilmore feels that attitudes within athletics are changing because
   A   coaches have begun to realise the importance of more intensive training.
   B   experts have begun to highlight the need for more unusual workouts.
   C   athletes are now being given mental as well as physical training by experts.
   D   coaches now encourage athletes to unwind between training sessions.

4   According to Dr. Wilmore, how are today's children different from years ago?
   A   They participate in far more sports.
   B   They begin sports at a much earlier age.
   C   They become more proficient in their chosen sports.
   D   They are more likely to become professional athletes.

5   Dr. Wilmore believes that women
   A   have physically developed and advanced over the years.
   B   perform equally well whether they are tall or short.
   C   now have the same chance as boys of realising their potential.
   D   are beginning to play sports at a much younger age than boys.

6   What conclusion does Dr. Wilmore make?
   A   We try to push the human body to its limits at our peril.
   B   We must congratulate ourselves on what athletes have achieved so far.
   C   We need to do more research into what the human body is capable of.
   D   We should not prejudge what might be beyond our physical capabilities.

English in Use

Part 4 Word formation

1 Read the two texts below quickly and decide which summary, a or b, is the most suitable.

A quick workout
a   A short workout is better than no workout.
b   A short workout is better than a long workout.

In love with science
a   Scientific research can explain the effects of romantic love.
b   Scientific research can explain the causes of romantic love.

2 Read both texts again and complete the gaps with words formed from 1–7 and 1–8.

a quick workout

For those with (0). insufficient time to spend hours working out in the gym, there is some good news. Researchers have found that fitness (1) .... can effectively reduce their workout time by two-thirds. And with gym (2) .... soaring in recent years, doctors are hoping the (3) .... will encourage even more people to take up exercise.

According to the results, it is not (4) .... to spend hours exercising when a shorter, more energetic workout achieves the same results. Those who exercised less saw a significant (5) .... in body fat. Participants had to reduce their exercise time, but increase the level of difficulty. Experts believe this proves that a streamlined exercise programme is more (6) .... and also gives you more free time.

Critics point out, however, that you need a good level of fitness before tackling exercise of such (7) ....

0 SUFFICIENT	4 PRODUCE
1 ENTHUSIASM	5 REDUCE
2 MEMBER	6 BENEFIT
3 FIND	7 INTENSE

IN LOVE WITH SCIENCE

The magic of head-over-heels love has just become a little less (0). mysterious thanks to the latest scientific research and its (1) .... images. Scientists have produced brain scans of people in the first stages of love and have arrived at an interesting (2) .... : romance is actually closer to (3) .... urges such as hunger or thirst than to excitement or affection. However, as a relationship (4) .... and continues, brain activity begins to change and can stimulate neural activity that represents long-term (5) ....

The research claims that when you experience romantic love, you can become out of control and completely (6) .... Under these conditions it is 'normal' to feel euphoria one minute, then anger and (7) .... the next, or even cause out-of-character behaviour, such as (8) .... phone-calling or singing serenades.

0 MYSTERY	5 ATTACH
1 REVOLUTION	6 RATIONAL
2 CONCLUDE	7 ANXIOUS
3 BIOLOGY	8 COMPEL
4 DEEP	

Would you believe it?

Reading

Part 1 and 4 Multiple matching

1 Read the text about superheroes. How does the writer ultimately feel about the characters in the films?

- inspired
- disappointed
- angry

2 In which section (A–F) of the text are 1–12 mentioned?

an assault on an innocent person	1 …	2 …
a seemingly endless collection of costumes	3 …	
a box-office hit for superheroes	4 …	
a heroine frightened of beginning relationships with men	5 …	
a summary of the drawbacks of being a superhero	6 …	7 …
a secret and harmful invention that is uncovered	8 …	
a heroine who seems to detest herself	9 …	
an expert that advises and guides a heroine	10 …	11 …
a search for something which causes global suffering	12 …	

CAN GIRLS BE SUPERHEROES?

A

Batman has flapped to the top of the charts, with $200m in his vault. Superman has put in yet another appearance; to those who inhabit out-of-town multiplexes, it is easy to believe that we are being held
5 hostage by larger-than-life male superheroes. If little boys have the bat and the alien that wears turquoise tights, who can little girls admire? I have a few hours to spare one night after work, so I head off in search of an inspirational female superhero at the DVD shop and
10 take out four films: *Catwoman*, *Elektra*, *Lara Croft Tomb Raider: The Cradle of Life* and *Charlie's Angels: Full Throttle*. They will have a heroine to send Batman back to his cave for me, won't they?

B

My first supergirl is Catwoman. Patience Philips, played
by Halle Berry, is a graphic designer at a cosmetics
company. When Patience discovers that evil genius
Laurel Hedare has designed a new face cream that will
make all Americans ugly, Hedare ensures that she
meets with a fatal accident. Although Patience dies, she
is reanimated by cats. She finds a guru who says,
'Catwomen are not contained by the rules of society.
You will often be lonely and misunderstood.' I begin to
despair. Catwoman, I decide, is a loser. She finds a cop
boyfriend and looks up at him adoringly. She steals a
shopful of jewellery and returns it in a paper bag
marked: 'Sorry'. Doesn't being a supergirl mean never
having to say you're sorry? She is also thick. Hedare
frames her for murder – easily. Kitty has to sob (to a
man!) to be released from jail. My finger trembles over
'Eject' but relents. Perhaps she'll improve. She doesn't.
Although she does succeed in rescuing the world from
killer face-cream, as the credits roll the boyfriend is
dumped and Patience pads into the moonlight alone.
This is not superheroic, it's a pathetic example of
unnecessary self-sacrifice.

C

My next potential idol is Elektra, from the 'supergirl'
class. Elektra is a reincarnated, knife-throwing, ninja
babe-assassin who can only stab people if she is
wearing a red satin bustier. 'Legend tells of a warrior –
a lost soul,' says a disembodied voice on the film. A
pattern is emerging here – a superheroine always has
to be lost; she gets good thighs but is denied street
maps. 'It is her destiny to tip the balance of good and
evil.' Elektra is not only lost, she is, according to mentor
Terence Stamp, 'poisoned by tragedy.' Even her
protector cannot protect her
from the truth. My heart
sinks. Elektra has an
obsessive compulsive
disorder and likes to
arrange bananas and
shampoo into rows.
She's bitter – 'Nobody
tells the truth about
themselves' – and her
dialogue is culled from
television scripts – 'My
mother died when I was
young. I should go. Thanks for
dinner.' Like Catwoman,
Elektra is not super enough
to have a functioning
relationship. When she
does kiss a man, she
panics. 'I'm not the kind of person you
should get involved with,' she sobs.

D

Another pattern seems to be emerging. At one point,
the villainous Hand breathes on Elektra's face and gives
her spots. In Superland, the worse thing you can do to
a superwoman (after making her a superwoman) is to
give her acne. Elektra triumphs over Hand but, like the
Cat, she pays the price and takes the fall. Just two films
in, the message to women from Hollywood is : You
want to be a superwoman? Are you sure? Well,
unhappiness is mandatory and being miserable, vital.
This is the sad reality of what you will have to endure
as a heroine. Elektra clearly does not like it and slumps
into a puddle of self-loathing. She stares at a ninja girl
of thirteen and whines: 'Please don't let her turn out
like me.'

E

The girls with supernatural powers were unsuper. So I
turn to the girls with superskills, beginning with Lara
Croft, as played by Angelina Jolie in *Lara Croft Tomb
Raider: The Cradle of Life*. Lara is like the girls I was at
school with: an ordinary suburban girl who talks like a
film actress and lives in a large house in the
countryside. Her quest is to find the mythical Pandora's
Box, the source of the world's grief, before evil scientists
get hold of it. She drives a motorbike along the Great
Wall of China and sky-dives off a bank, but then 'The
Message' pops up again. 'You're afraid of letting anyone
in,' says her boyfriend. Lara shoots him, without any
apparent justification, then strikes the pose of a noble
superheroine-in-solitude. Do you understand, ladies?
Superwoman can't have a super relationship or super
contentment and the pay-off for her super gift is
isolation, loneliness, misanthropy and, eventually, no
doubt, contracting some ghastly disease in her old age.

F

My quest for a superwoman ends with *Charlie's
Angels: Full Throttle*. In scene one, the Angels,
wearing very tight clothes, get rid off a gaggle of
cheery gangsters. They return to LA, to serve their
patriarch Charlie –an elusive man who delivers their
orders, assists from afar, and congratulates them at
appropriate moments – and are informed they
have to recover some important data for
the FBI. I watch as they succeed with a
combination of looking gorgeous, karate,
and disco-dancing. They change their outfits
practically every thirty
seconds and wear aquamarine
mascara and, after two hours, the
Angels see off baddie Demi Moore.
It is certainly not heroic. My TV screams for
mercy. My girls-night-out in Superland is over.
Under their masks, I saw only weakness.
Batman has won.

Vocabulary

The truth

1 Choose the best answer (A, B or C) to complete sentences 1–6.

1 John .... to me about winning the cycle race – he actually came third.
   A lay   B lied   C has lain

2 The accused tried in vain to .... the true nature of the crime he had committed.
   A conceal   B shelter   C protect

3 We have evidence to prove that the new car was paid for with .... money.
   A copy   B counterfeit   C mock

4 We have complete .... in the government's ability to solve problems of unemployment.
   A loyalty   B honour   C faith

5 Stuart managed to .... everyone in with elaborate stories of his childhood.
   A have   B put   C take

6 You can rely on Elizabeth to give you good advice. I'd .... her judgement every time.
   A trust   B presume   C assume

Words with similar meanings (2)

2 Match words 1–3 with definitions a or b.

1 snigger / giggle
   a laugh in an unpleasant way at someone
   b laugh in a silly way (often young people)

2 whisper / mumble
   a speak quietly and very unclearly
   b speak quietly so only some people can hear

3 eavesdrop / overhear
   a accidentally hear a conversation
   b secretly listen to a conversation

3 Use the correct form of words from 2 in these sentences.

a How do you know about that? You must have been .... We haven't told anyone yet!

b All the students .... nervously as they waited for their test results to be announced.

c Try not to .... when you speak. No one can hear you properly.

Meanings of *hold*

4 Complete sentences 1–6 with a suitable phrase from the ones below.

■ for questioning   responsible   a party
  extreme views   my attention   the line

1 Teachers will be *held* .... for the behaviour of pupils in their class.

2 Two men were *held* .... in connection with the break-ins in the area.

3 I enjoyed the play but it didn't *hold* .... as much as the playwright's last one.

4 The election result was surprising as the winning candidate *held* ....

5 We're going to *hold* .... next month.

6 Can you *hold* .... and I'll put you through?

5 Match the examples of *hold* from 4 with the different meanings or uses below.

a wait momentarily
b be liable
c put on
d detain
e possess
f keep/maintain

Grammar

Modals

1 Circle the most suitable modal in these sentences.

a You *shouldn't/mustn't* have wasted your time typing out the letter. You knew we weren't going to send it.

b A work permit *must/need* be obtained in advance by anyone intending to live and reside in the country.

c You *need/should* always seek advice before signing any legal documentation.

d The staff *must/should* be very contented working here. Everyone has a smile on their face.

e I suppose your order *might/can* have been lost. These things can happen.

f I'm afraid I *can't/shouldn't* make out what the writing on this prescription says – it's illegible.

g You *ought to/need* think carefully before making any decision.

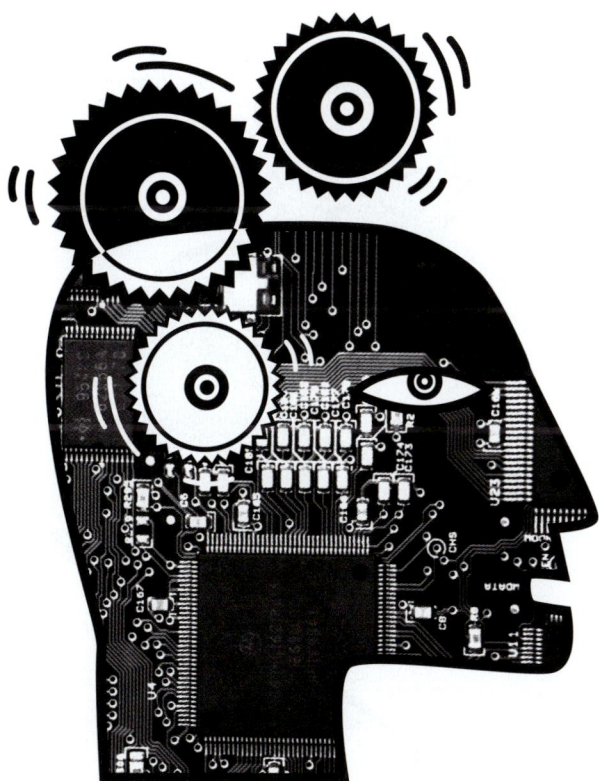

2 Complete these sentences using modals of assumption or deduction and the correct form of one of the verbs below.

■ miss   delay   receive   be   pass   do

a She <u>must have passed</u> the exam – look, she's smiling and laughing!

b The hotel .... our booking as they had no reservation under the name 'Wright'.

c It's odd that James hasn't arrived yet – do you think his plane .... ?

d I think you .... him actually, he's normally gone by this time.

e You .... well at the interview, otherwise they wouldn't have offered you the job!

f Surely Sally .... serious when she said she was going to sell all her possessions and go and live on a desert island?

3 Match the modals in a–c with meanings 1–3.

a Visitors needn't return the museum catalogue – it's theirs to keep.

b Passengers with season tickets don't need to purchase tickets on a daily basis.

c I needn't have called directory enquiries. I had the number in my diary after all.

1 It was done, but it was not necessary.
2 It is not necessary, but can be done (if required).
3 This is not necessary.

4 Complete sentences a–d with *needn't* or *needn't have* and one of the correct form of the verbs in brackets.

a 'I stayed up late revising, but when I saw the exam paper, I realised I .... (worry)!'

b 'You .... (pay) anything now. A bill will be sent to you in due course.'

c 'Apparently fans .... (arrive) early for the concert – there will be plenty of available seats.'

d 'We .... (spend) all that time looking for a bank – there was a cash machine here!'

Listening

Part 4 Multiple choice

1 You will hear five people talking about popular beliefs connected with food. Do you think these comments are true or false?

- Breakfast is the most important meal of the day.
- Eating carrots helps you see in the dark.
- Eating fish will make you more clever.

2 🎧 Now listen to the five people and choose the best answer (A, B or C) for 1–10.

1 The first speaker says the results of American studies into breakfast in 1950 were
   A initially regarded with suspicion.
   B believed to be completely reliable.
   C supported by subsequent research.

2 What does he think about eating breakfast?
   A It makes no different to how he feels.
   B He enjoys breakfast mid-morning.
   C It's a desirable part of his daily routine.

3 The second speaker implies that popular beliefs about eating carrots
   A are absolutely true.
   B are completely unfounded.
   C are based on well-researched evidence.

4 She believes that eating carrots
   A can actually help people to see in the dark.
   B makes little difference to many people's sight.
   C will provide valuable vitamin supplements.

5 The third speaker says that the cartoon character Popeye
   A misled parents into believing that spinach is good for you.
   B made spinach extremely popular for a short time.
   C was used to encouraged children to eat spinach.

6 He implies that people are not aware that
   A cooked spinach is better for you than raw spinach.
   B the iron in spinach is difficult to absorb when eaten on its own.
   C oranges and peppers contain more vitamins than spinach.

7 What did the fourth speaker think about her mother's remedies for colds and fevers?
   A They were the only real cure for the illnesses.
   B There was no truth in them.
   C They were comforting when she was a child.

8 She says that recent research into colds
   A will eventually provide a cure for the common cold.
   B has helped us to decide what to eat when we have a cold.
   C has proved that eating helps you fight a cold.

9 How does the fifth speaker feel about eating fish?
   A It's not one of his favourite types of food.
   B He is glad he enjoys it because it's good for you.
   C He totally refused to eat it as a child.

10 What comment does he make about eating oily fish?
   A It really can make you more intelligent.
   B It helps the brain to develop in infancy.
   C It can help you lose weight if you are on a diet.

English in Use

Part 5 Register transfer

1 Read the newspaper article about a problem with the lack of sunlight in an Italian village. What is the possible solution?

2 Read the article again, then use the information in it to complete gaps 1–13 in the letter. Use no more than two words per gap.

Giant mirror to light up mountainside

The Mayor of Viganella, a village in the Italian Alps, has proposed erecting a giant mirror on a nearby mountainside to reflect sunlight into the village square. It may sound far-fetched, but the scheme would try to counteract a serious local case of 'Seasonal Affective Disorder'. From November to February, the sun vanishes behind a mountain ridge, plunging the village and its inhabitants into gloom. The mirror, powered by an electric motor, would rotate to track the path of the sun and reflect rays towards the village. This will transform the small piazza into an area bathed in sunlight and warmth.

'For us, the rationale is obvious,' explains Mayor Midali. 'It would have a good psychological effect on the population and we would have a spot where we could socialise.' He added that a study had been conducted and plans had then been drafted. 'We have been very aware of not interfering with the beauty of the countryside. The mirror will be concealed in woods so will not even be visible.'

The only drawback in making this a reality is that while the mayor has pledged to contribute a fifth of the €94,000 costs from local funds, provincial authorities have so far denied them the rest.

Dear Paul,

Thought you might be interested in a story I came across in the paper the other day. Apparently the mayor of a village in the Italian Alps has 0 .....suggested..... putting up a huge mirror on the side of a mountain which will throw sunlight back into the village. It's no joke! The idea is meant to 1 .... the depression people feel because of a lack of sunlight. For four months in winter, the sun just 2 .... behind the mountains. They are going to use an electric motor powerful enough to 3 .... the mirror which will then catch the sunlight. This will 4 .... the town centre completely – it will be warm and sunny!

The 5 .... for doing this are clear; it would make everyone feel 6 .... and people would have somewhere to 7 .... friends. They've already 8 .... a study and 9 .... a plan. They've been careful not to do anything which might 10 .... the beautiful countryside and the mirror will be 11 .... by the woods. But there is just one small 12 .... – the mayor has 13 .... to provide one fifth of the money needed but the authorities have not come up with the rest!

Review Units 4–6

1 Replace the words in italics with a suitable expression containing one of these words.

■ hand   head   tongue   fingers   foot

a I *offended someone unintentionally* when I criticised the meal. I didn't realise Sue had cooked it.
b I'm starving. Let's *go to* the nearest restaurant.
c Can anyone *help me* to carry these books to the library?
d There must be more to life than *working hard or for long hours* every day.
e What was that film we saw last week? *I can't remember at the moment.*

2 Correct the six mistakes with past tenses in this paragraph.

Example
University students ~~had~~ **have** made it their mission to save the Iberian lynx from extinction by undertaking a sponsored walk.

The students have become aware of the plight of the lynx when they had been starting some research into various species as part of their course. It has appeared that the lynx had being threatened by several factors. In recent years, their numbers were been depleted and their natural habitat has decreasing.

3 Complete sentences a–f with a suitable word.

a Police have discovered that *counterfeit/copy* money was used to pay for the goods.
b Remember that whenever you need help, you can *count/calculate* on me.
c I have to confess that I deliberately *overheard/eavesdropped* an extremely interesting conversation yesterday.
d The con man managed to *take/put* us in with his lies.
e What are you two *whispering/mumbling* about? What's the big secret?
f Kate could be an excellent student but spends too much time *sniggering/giggling* at silly jokes in the class.

4 Match sentence halves a –f with 1–6.

a A general election will be …
b The film didn't …
c Three men have been …
d Students will be …
e I don't think this good weather will …
f Although the political group …

1 hold my attention at all.
2 held responsible for keeping their classroom clean and tidy.
3 held next month.
4 held for questioning in connection with obtaining money under false pretences.
5 hold rather radical views, they have a large following.
6 hold for much longer.

5 Correct any incorrect negative prefixes in a–i.

a insteady   ....
b unviolent   ....
c unfortunate   ....
d inprecise   ....
e illegal   ....
f innatural   ....
g misorganised   ....
h non-understood   ....
i dispronounced   ....

6 Read the text below and correct the four mistakes with modals.

Jane Henley would not be happier after winning in the international field and track event at the age of 19. Her parents might have been delighted with her success. It mustn't have been easy making the sacrifices necessary for their daughter to realise her dream. They admitted they were very nervous, however, they needn't have worry!

7 Complete the dialogues using *a*, *an*, *the* or no article.

1 A: Do you ever travel to work by .... train?
   B: Never – I prefer to go by .... bus or on .... foot.

2 A: What can .... governments do to help .... unemployed?
   B: They can increase .... unemployment benefits for .... start.

3 A: What do you think is .... main difference between .... British and .... French?
   B: Probably .... food they eat.

4 A: Were you at .... work when you heard .... news about the earthquake?
   B: I was at .... home watching TV.

5 A: I'll pick you up after .... dinner and we'll go to .... cinema.
   B: Fine – we'll have finished .... meal by about 7.30.

6 A: What does Jim want to do when he leaves .... school?
   B: He wants to join .... police force.

7 A: Do you have .... favourite flower?
   B: Yes – it's .... orchid.

8 A: What do you consider to be .... greatest invention ever?
   B: .... computer, of course.

8 Complete the adjectives below, then use these adjectives in sentences a–f.

suspic..............   inform..............
court..............   malic..............
outrag..............   terr..............

a David is extremely charming. I've never met anyone so .... and polite.

b If you're confused about technology, read this book. It's .... and really useful.

c The candidate failed to win due to the .... rumours the opposition had spread.

d That film was .... It's the worst I've seen for ages.

e What's that man doing? He's behaving in a very .... manner.

f She's one of the world's most .... singers and always causes controversy.

9 Rewrite this dialogue in indirect speech using the correct form of the reporting verbs in a–f. More than one answer may be possible.

Example

TED: What motivated you to become a safari guide?

Ted asked Sarah what had motivated her to become a safari guide. (ask)

SARAH: Ever since I was a child, I've been desperate to travel.

a .... (admit)
Have you ever been on safari?

b .... (ask)
TED: No, I haven't.

c .... (tell)
But it is one of my ambitions.

d .... (add)
SARAH: I hope one day you will go on one.

e .... (go on to say)
Why don't you take a place on my next trip?

f .... (offer)

10 Correct nouns a–e to make nouns for a person.

a terroriser   ....
b coordinater   ....
c immigrator   ....
d survivant   ....
e observist   ....

Traces of the past

Reading Part 2 Gapped text

1 Read the text and paragraphs A–G to find out which city is being described and when it was founded.

2 Read the whole text again and match paragraphs A–G with gaps 1–6. There is one extra paragraph.

A city of many faces

She used to be the Queen of the Deep South. An aristocratic party girl decked in jewels. She could be charming and romantic. She could be corrupt and racist. She had jazz rhythms beating in
5 her heart. She was called 'the city that care forgot'. But in 2005 the city died, drowned beneath the flood waters of a hurricane called Katrina.

1 ....

Louis Armstrong sang the old favourite, 'Do you know what it means to miss New Orleans?' In the
10 summer of 2005, the population found out. Previously the city had swung to a different rhythm from the rest of the world. Mardi Gras turned it into an annual event of over-indulgence every February; a party atmosphere that lingered.

2 ....

15 The city also looked different from others. Its blend of French and Spanish created an architecture of European elegance unseen elsewhere in the US, rivalling Paris and Madrid. But in 2005, the historic wooden homes were rotting under water: a living
20 museum that was perhaps destined for the bulldozers. It seemed a tragic end for a city that always knew that it lived in the shadow of rising waters, on land borrowed from the sea.

3 ....

For ten years before that, its residents were quite
25 varied. A community of fur trappers lived on the one piece of high ground nestled along the flood-prone banks of the lower Mississippi river. And the British occupied the Eastern seaboard, while the French were claiming the South. Named in honour of the
30 Duke of Orleans, Regent of France, the city became the capital of French Louisiana.

4 ....

It proved to be a bargain. Sitting beside the great Mississippi, only 100 miles north of the open waters of the Gulf, the city quickly became a thriving
35 economic powerhouse and the fourth largest city in America. It became a leading port and a large Creole population with Spanish or French ancestry brought their own unique flavours to the city in more ways than one.

5 ....

40 New Orleans will always remain a city steeped in memories for millions of those tourists. It was loved for its diversity and its tolerance, for its chicory-flavoured sweet, dark coffee, and its broad, slow-paced southern drawl. It always maintained its sense
45 of nobility, high-minded civility and air of historic superiority. It was a town of great luxury and privilege, but it was also something of a paradox.

6 ....

But whatever the city's merits and defects, the one question on everyone's mind in 2005 was: 'Can New
50 Orleans rise again?'

A Its cultural melting pot brought not only its own language but also its own cuisine. In recent years, this became popular on an international level and has even spread to the finest restaurants worldwide.
55 Perhaps this even contributed to its universal appeal to 'wanna-be' visitors.

B The unfortunate city was New Orleans – built from the swamps and rivers of southern Louisiana – and that summer, the city was reclaimed by them.
60 Beneath the murky waters lay a city that one day might be drained, salvaged and rebuilt but one which had, for the moment at least, lost much of its unique heritage, architecture and spirit.

C Beneath its façade of gentility, its hands were as
65 dirty as the rich deep mud of the Mississippi delta. Corruption and racism stood alongside great poverty, high crime and unemployment in many of its African-American suburbs.

D The land reclamation opened up much of the city to
70 new construction but meant that even heavy rains had to be rapidly pumped away before the city was inundated. Once recovered, it continued to establish itself as a popular tourist destination with visitors coming from all over the world, all seeking to enjoy
75 the many and varied characteristics of a unique city.

E It was indeed a place surrounded by water – alligator-infested marshy swamps and the tidal waters from the Gulf of Mexico. But this did not stop the French explorer Jean-Baptiste Le Moyne de
80 Bienville founding it in 1718.

F At the beginning of the nineteenth century, Napoleon sold a large part of the continent, including New Orleans and parts of a dozen modern states, to the United States in the Louisiana Purchase
85 for $15 million – the equivalent of about $193 million today.

G Music flowed through its veins, not just for one-off festivities, but throughout the year. It permeated the plush clubs and the street corners of the French
90 Quarter, from the old men with weathered faces playing in the bare and sombre Preservation Hall, to the defiant swing of the musicians marching in a funeral cortege. Its culture was clearly not that of your average city.

Vocabulary

Phrasal verbs with *off* and *in*

1 Complete 1–5 with phrasal verbs formed from these verbs plus *off*.

    take   bring   call   cut   show

1 During winter, the mountain villages are often .... by heavy snowstorms.
2 No-one expected Colin to organise the end-of-term party by himself, but he managed to .... it ....
3 Ted thinks he knows everything – he's always .... his expertise in something or other.
4 Plans for the wedding were unfortunately .... at the last minute as the bride fell in love with the best man.
5 Peterson's career really .... following the huge box-office hit of his first feature film.

2 Match the phrasal verbs from 1 with meanings a–e below.

a end suddenly and unexpectedly
b succeed against expectations
c begin to be successful
d to be isolated
e try to impress people

3 Use the correct form of the verbs from 1 with the particle *in* to complete dialogues 1–5 below.

1 A: That's terrible – you must feel absolutely awful!
  B: I just can't believe it. I had to read his letter again and again to ....
2 A: Are you ready to talk to the candidates?
  B: Yes. Will you please .... them .... now?
3 A: Why were the police .... ?
  B: To investigate allegations of bribery and corruption.
4 A: More should be done to help one-parent families.
  B: But the government has only recently .... new measures to help them.
5 A: Have you met Andy's cousin? He's very rude.
  B: You can say that again. He always .... whenever someone tries to speak.

4 Match the phrasal verbs from 3 with meanings a–e below.

a introduce
b bring here
c try to understand the meaning
d interrupt
e request to come and help

5 Choose the correct particle in sentences a–e to make a two-part phrasal verb.

a If you are told *in/off*, you have upset someone by doing something wrong or badly.
b If you take someone *in/off*, you let them stay at your house.
c If you go *in/off* something, don't like it anymore.
d If you keep something *in/off*, you prevent yourself from saying what you think.
e If something pulls people *in/off*, it makes a lot of people want to see it.

Grammar

Participle clauses

1 Complete the encyclopedia entry below using the correct participle form of the verbs in brackets.

The Atacama desert

1 .... (lie) between the high mountains of the Andes and the Pacific Ocean, and 2 .... (locate) in the northern part of Chile, the desert is the perfect terrain for preservation. 3 .... (bury) in the sand in prehistoric times, bodies can remain almost intact as mummies.

4 .... (receive) less than 0.02 centimetres of rain a year – with some parts 5 .... (not/see) rainfall for the last 400 years – the Atacama desert is the most arid tract of land 6 .... (know). The area is favoured by scientists 7 .... (search) for the presence of water.

Grammar Extra

Suffixes

2 Match groups a–h with a suitable suffix. Remember you may have to change the spelling.

◼ ess hood ship ness ist less ese ful ee

a train / employ / attend
b friend / relation / owner
c steward / act / host
d child / neighbour / likely
e happy / like / sweet
f special / capital / art
g care / hope / rest
h China / Portugal / Lebanon

3 Which group from 2 can take two suffixes?

4 Complete sentences a–l with the words in brackets and one of the suffixes below.

◼ ian cy ment ty

a (politics) Only one .... decided to back the revaluation of the currency yesterday.
b (content) They say that secret of .... lies in leading a simple life.
c (anxious) The selection process caused great .... in applicants for the job.
d (music) Even a talented .... can have problems finding work.
e (clear) One of the most important qualities of effective writing is ....
f (fulfil) Vocational jobs such as teaching can bring great ....
g (democratic) .... means government by the people for the people.
h (argue) It is often difficult to make up after a heated ....
i (technical) Unfortunately the .... was unable to repair the computer.
j (secret) Each committee member must be sworn to .... prior to the ceremony.
k (authentic) Experts consider the .... of the manuscript to be under serious doubt.
l (diplomatic) Tact and .... are skills that are not easily learned.

Listening

Part 2 Sentence completion

1 What do you already know about life for humans in prehistoric times?

2 🎧 Listen to someone talking about the oldest intact skeleton ever found in England, and complete sentences 1–9.

a prehistoric family

9,000 years ago, south-eastern England was linked to Europe by .... (1).

'Cheddar Man' was discovered in a cave surrounded by bones from .... (2).

Radiocarbon dating has shown that Cheddar Man dates back to .... (3) BC.

He moved across north-western Europe in a .... (4).

Cheddar Man's main food supply was .... (5).

It was an injury to the .... (6) that caused his death.

A study was made of one of the .... (7) belonging to the skeleton.

Adrian Targett, a teacher of .... (8), was a close DNA match of 'Cheddar Man'.

Despite .... (9) from many different nationalities, Targett's family remained in Cheddar Gorge.

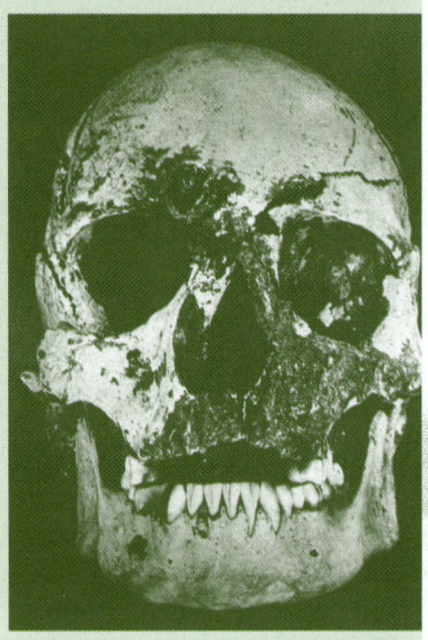

English in Use

Part 4 Word formation

1 Read the texts below quickly and answer these questions.

Port Royal

a What is the past simple of *sink*? What is the past participle?

b Would you try to *raise* or *rise* a wreck from the seabed?

c What adjective is formed from *adventure*?

The Terra-Cotta Army

d What is the difference in meaning between *found* and *founded*?

e What adjective is formed from *watch*?

f What noun is formed from *real*?

2 Read both texts again and complete the gaps with words formed from 1–7 and 1–8.

PORT ROYAL

In the seventeenth century, Port Royal was a 0 *legendary* city of vast wealth. Today, it is remembered for the 1692 earthquake and tidal wave that caused it to sink beneath the sea, and it is the subject of many books.

Robert F. Marx's book is the latest example; in it he describes the 1 .... of his dream – the exploration of this historic Jamaican port. 2 .... speaking, this was the first investigation by a trained marine archaeologist, and he discovered thousands of perfectly preserved artefacts.

Port Royal did not give up its treasures easily however: working on an 3 .... tight budget, Marx had to cope with 4 .... problems, such as polluted waters, sharks, and tough 5 .... from financial and political interests.

Blending real-life adventure and impressive 6 .... descriptions, Marx has written an 7 .... account of one of the most important marine expeditions ever undertaken.

0 LEGEND	4 END
1 FULFIL	5 OPPOSE
2 SCIENCE	6 VISION
3 BELIEVE	7 INFORM

The Terra-Cotta Army

The clay figures of the Terra-Cotta Army that guard the tomb of the first Chinese Emperor, Qin Shihuang, were found 1 .... by Chinese peasants while digging a well. Further 2 .... showed that the warriors had been placed around the tomb after the Emperor's 3 ....

During his reign there were three attempts to 4 .... him. This may explain why, despite being only thirteen when he came to power, he immediately made 5 .... for an underground tomb to be built for his death.

The figures guarding the tomb were made one at a time. Each soldier had an 6 .... individualistic face, probably the 7 .... of a real soldier. For more than 2,000 years, these soldiers have kept a 8 .... watch over the tomb.

1 ACCIDENT	5 ARRANGE
2 EXCAVATE	6 MISTAKE
3 BURY	7 LIKE
4 ASSASSIN	8 CONTINUE

The big issues

Reading Part 3 Multiple choice

1 Read the text about a new computer program and find out what it aims to do.
Is it successful?

WE'RE FUNNY IN THE BRAIN

A computer walks into a bar ... no, hang on, why did the mainframe computer cross the road? Please, don't groan. Information Technology (IT) humour doesn't work very well. Computers don't do jokes and the people who
5 understand computers aren't famous for being a load of laughs either. But Dr Binsted, an expert in Artificial Intelligence (AI), plans to change that. If her project succeeds, your computer of the future could be swapping puns (jokes on word play) and wisecracks with you faster
10 than a New York cab driver.

Binsted is one of the speakers on humour, art and the brain, at the Festival of Art and the Mind, in England. She will unveil a computer program called 'WISCRAIC' (Witty Idiomatic Sentence Creation Revealing Ambiguity in
15 Context) which will entertain the audience with its stock of clever jokes. However, since examples include 'The book thief was caught read-handed instead of 'red-handed', it's obvious that Binsted's cyber comedian cannot be relied upon for its ability to make people laugh.
20 But that is one reason why the project is so interesting. The fact that *Wiscraic* and his punning companion *Jape* (Joke Analysis Production Engine) find even basic humour so hard, despite access to vast language databases, is a vivid demonstration of what a difficult thing humour is.

25 They are certainly nowhere near answering the most fundamental question – why do human beings laugh and make jokes at all? Why is it that whenever two or three people are gathered together, we smile and send out a series of short noises, each about 75 milliseconds long,
30 repeated at regular intervals? One rather surprising answer is social dominance.

When researcher Professor Provine, at the University of Maryland, eavesdropped in clubs and bars to find exactly what happens when people laugh, he discovered that it is
35 something women do in response to men. When talking to men, women will laugh 127 per cent more than their male audience, while men talking to a female audience will laugh seven per cent less than their audience. 'Laughter, like many other social activities, is connected with status
40 and the desire of the male to impress,' Provine says. 'Top people don't laugh; you laugh at what they say.' Both male and female listeners laugh more when a man is speaking, but in neither case do the jokes have to be any good.

But when we laugh at something that is funny, what goes
45 on in our brains? Understanding this is the ultimate dream of neuroscience because while we can locate memories, speech and even religious experiences in the brain, jokes turn out to be even more complex. Neuroscientists have known for some years that if you damage the right side of
50 your brain, story-telling jokes of the 'Man walks into a bar' variety are lost on you – but comedy based on clumsy actions or embarrassing situations is guaranteed a laugh. When subjects were recently put in a scanner at the Institute of Neurology in London and told a popular joke,
55 an area at the back of their frontal lobes was activated. But a rather different picture emerged when researchers at the institute told subjects puns or what they called 'semantic jokes' – 'Why don't sharks bite lawyers?' 'Professional courtesy.' While both types amused the part
60 of the brain which deals with reward and control, they arrived there via different routes. The puns went through an area that controls speech (the Broca's), while the 'semantic' jokes went through the temporal lobes.

So it's obvious that humour is, in fact, a serious matter,
65 with a strong social dimension that needs a surprising amount of brain power and a willingness to break rules. Attempting to programme these requirements into a computer sounds unrealistic at best. 'It's true that in science fiction robots can usually do everything – except
70 make jokes,' Binsted says, 'but one of the aims of AI is

to model what humans do and to replicate it.' She defends Wiscraic's playground jokes with an analogy about computer-composed music. 'It goes all the way from the sophisticated music of Beethoven down to
75 short, simple tunes in adverts and right now we are still at the advertising end! But it's a start. If computers are going to interact with humans via language, they are going to have to do humour.' What's intriguing is just how unsuccessful the computer is – 'The friendly
80 gardener had thyme (a garden herb, as opposed to time) for the women' – compared with the real thing, like Groucho Marx's 'I have had a perfectly wonderful evening. But this wasn't it.' Why exactly one works perfectly and the others make everyone groan is the
85 kind of question that keeps academics in work for decades.

But already Binsted's joking computer has its fans in at least one place where language is highly valued. It is currently being used to teach English to Japanese

90 students who can chat with a screen. The program makes a joke like the 'friendly gardener' one and then deconstructs it to explain the idiomatic use of the word *time*. 'We've found that students remember more and keep working longer when the screen throws up the
95 occasional joke,' Binsted says.

2 Read the text again and choose the correct answer (A, B, C or D) to questions 1–6.

1 What statement does the writer make in the first paragraph?
A There are numerous jokes about the computer industry.
B IT people often make up amusing jokes about computers.
C Some computers are capable of making up their own jokes.
D The IT industry is not well-known for its sense of humour.

2 According to the writer, the computer program called *Wiscraic*
A has been programmed to understand the real meaning of humour.
B has a long way to go before it succeeds in its comic aims.
C would greatly benefit from more access to language databases.
D is capable of making large numbers of people laugh hysterically.

3 One explanation for why humans laugh in certain situations is that it
A helps them demonstrate their position in society.
B provides a welcome change of pace in conversations.
C enables people to establish closer contact with one another.
D is a means of showing appreciation of what we find funny.

4 Scientists have only recently discovered that
A damage to the right brain can interfere with our understanding of jokes.
B people find puns and semantic jokes more appealing than ordinary jokes.
C the brain processes different kinds of jokes in different ways.
D programming a computer to process jokes like humans would be impossible.

5 Binsted compares Wiscraic to computer-composed music in order to
A prove how capable the computerised humour program is.
B show how computerised humour is still in its infancy.
C illustrate the skills needed by humans to match computerised humour.
D highlight the number of academics involved in the humour project.

6 What happened when Wiscraic was used as a tool for teaching English to Japanese students?
A It caused minor problems for some of the students.
B The students understood the jokes immediately.
C A teacher had to be present to explain the jokes.
D The jokes helped the students become more effective in their studies.

Vocabulary

Compound adjectives

1 Match groups a–e with 1–5 to make compound adjectives.

a   half-/light-/down   1   minded
b   open-/narrow-/broad-   2   made
c   full-/part-/first-   3   handed
d   left-/right-/single-   4   hearted
e   man-/hand/self-   5   time

2 Use compound adjectives from 1 to complete sentences a–e. More than one answer may be possible.

a   Due to current expansion, there are vacancies for two .... members of staff.
b   These scissors are specially designed to be used by .... people.
c   The new play at the Criterion theatre is a .... look at life in suburbia.
d   He's extremely .... and always keen to hear what others think.
e   Have you seen these necklaces? They are all .... in Chile!

Negative adjectives

3 Write the opposites of words a–h using a <u>negative</u> prefix.

a   penetrable   impenetrable
b   tolerable   ....
c   perceptible   ....
d   reversible   ....
e   sensitive   ....
f   stable   ....
g   measurable   ....
h   sociable   ....

4 Match the <u>opposites</u> from 3 with the meanings in 1–8 below.

1   uncaring
2   incalculable
3   insecure
4   inhospitable
5   indistinguishable
6   unbearable
7   inaccessible
8   unchangeable

5 Complete sentences a–h with a suitable adjective from exercises 3 or 4.

a   Which of these paintings is the original? They're completely .... to me.
b   They're quite an .... family. They never really go out and mix with anyone.
c   The heat is .... in here. I can't believe the air conditioning is still broken.
d   Due to torrential weather conditions the mountain pass is .... via this route.
e   My little sister is still quite .... and always seems to feel self-conscious.
f   There are very few decisions in life that are .... in my experience.
g   Torrel's work is known throughout the world – his contribution to the arts is ....
h   I don't want to sound .... but it's time you sorted out your own mistakes!

Grammar

Conditionals

1 Look at the picture of the man and complete sentences a–e with a suitable conditional phrase using the verb in brackets.

Example

He would not have slipped (slip) if he hadn't gone so close to the edge.

a If he shouts for help, no one .... (hear) him.

b If he .... (take) a photo, he wouldn't be in trouble!

c If he could reach his mobile, he .... (call) for help.

d If he .... (reach) the tree, he could climb to safety.

e If he had told someone where he was, they .... (find) him.

2 Rewrite these conditional sentences using the prompts given.

a My aunt lent me the money, so I was able to go abroad.
If my aunt ....

b Never stay out in the midday sun because of the risk of getting burned.
If you ....

c Thomas had three jobs over the summer and then he was able to buy a motorbike.
If Thomas ....

d It's not certain that I can offer you a scholarship, but I'd like to know how you feel about it.
If I were ....

e Profits are down because demand for our products is falling.
If demand ....

3 Complete these conditional sentences using the correct form of the verb in brackets.

a When petrol .... (ignite), it .... (go up) in flames.

b If I .... (know) the answer to your question, I .... (tell) you.

c I .... (gain) lots of experience if I .... (volunteer) for the project – but I didn't apply.

d If visibility .... (not/be) poor last night, the flight .... (leave) on time.

e .... (let) me know if you .... (like) me to cook dinner tonight.

f If Jack .... (not/work) so hard at university, he .... (not/get) such a good degree.

Listening Part 3 Multiple choice

1 What do you already know about 'artificial intelligence'? Do you think these developments in technology are important for our lives?

2 🎧 Listen to a radio interview with Paul Williams, an expert in artificial intelligence, and choose the best answers for questions 1–7.

1 Paul explains that predictions made about AI in the past
   A turned out to be surprisingly accurate.
   B proved to be a long way off-target.
   C overestimated the demand for computers.
   D underestimated the 'brain power' of computers.

2 According to Paul, how do most experts feel about the future of AI?
   A convinced it could soon govern every aspect of our lives
   B uncertain what impact it might eventually have on our lives
   C worried that its development may get out of control
   D certain that its full effects will not be seen for some time yet

3 Paul defines 'narrow AI' as the type of AI which
   A an intelligent adult can understand.
   B is also being operated by human beings.
   C operates in a defined situation.
   D operates on small computers.

4 Paul feels that the comparison of AI and the arrival of the computer industry
   A shows that both industries are at a similar state of development.
   B illustrates that the computer industry was more popular in its time than AI.
   C misrepresents the true role of AI in our lives.
   D proves that the computer industry was a much more profitable concern.

5 What does Paul believe people's attitudes were to new technology in the 1900s?
   A They were very excited about its potential.
   B They had little idea what impact it would have.
   C They were suspicious of how it might change their lives.
   D They expected it to develop more quickly than it did.

6 Paul is slightly worried by the fact that machines which have intelligence could
   A one day kill off human beings.
   B rapidly assume human roles.
   C eventually replace humans in the workplace.
   D be running our lives in the near future.

7 What conclusion does Paul finally reach?
   A Science fiction is closer to reality than we think.
   B Intelligent machines will be able to feel emotions.
   C AI will develop more rapidly than we can ever imagine.
   D We should not be afraid that technology will take over our lives.

English in Use Part 1 Multiple-choice cloze

1 Read the article below, ignoring the gaps, about a survey into volunteering. Why do people and businesses want to become involved?

2 Read the article again and decide which word (A, B, C or D) best fits each space.

WHAT'S IN IT FOR ME?

Students and jobseekers keen to get onto the course or into the workplace of their (0) ...*B*... , hope that voluntary work will help them (1) .... from the crowd. This chance to (2) .... experience – personally and professionally – is (3) .... on the wish-list of young people.

A survey carried out last year revealed that young and old (4) .... said volunteering had improved their lives, particularly those (5) .... in conservation or heritage work.

Businesses recognise its importance and get to (6) .... their profile in the community, while staff get a break (7) .... their daily routine to develop 'soft skills', (8) .... initiative and decision-making. A volunteering organisation is (9) .... another survey to find out if volunteering does make a (10) .... in the workplace, or if it is something businesses do simply to improve their (11) ....

Not (12) .... are business-sponsored placements becoming more common, the government is also investing money and aiming to (13) .... volunteers. The push is clearly on to make volunteering as (14) .... as possible to everyone. And the more people who participate, the more the act fulfils its (15) .... of making the world a better place.

0	A alternative	B	choice	C	option	D	election
1	A stand out	B	lift out	C	pick out	D	point out
2	A win	B	achieve	C	collect	D	gain
3	A extreme	B	high	C	sharp	D	strong
4	A similar	B	the same	C	alike	D	too
5	A committed	B	associated	C	connected	D	involved
6	A raise	B	increase	C	arouse	D	motivate
7	A out	B	from	C	away	D	off
8	A such	B	such as	C	such like	D	such and such
9	A governing	B	guiding	C	conducting	D	directing
10	A mark	B	result	C	effect	D	difference
11	A representation	B	look	C	image	D	figure
12	A only	B	just	C	merely	D	simply
13	A claim	B	recruit	C	bring	D	enter
14	A charming	B	pleasing	C	attractive	D	preferable
15	A aim	B	direction	C	mark	D	design

It's a crime

Reading

Parts 1 and 4 Multiple matching

1 Quickly read the text about book reviews and find out in which country each novel is set.

2 Read the text again and decide in which paragraph (A–F) the following are mentioned.

a protagonist who fears he/she may be killed	1 … 2 …
the best novel the writer has written so far	3 …
a desire to make international literature more accessible	4 …
a novel that is impossible to stop reading	5 …
an era which is accurately captured by the writer	6 …
a crime against a family of considerable importance	7 …
a storyline that deliberately misleads the reader	8 …
a residence that is no longer appealing	9 …
a character who can move between social classes	10 … 11 …
a more optimistic story than the author usually writes	12 …
a protagonist who wishes to have a say in politics	13 …

'Really quite wonderful. I am a true fan.'
Michael Connelly

FAMILIES

A

In Denise Mina's *The Field of Blood*, it's 1981 and Paddy Meeham, eighteen, is determined that her lowly job as a copygirl on a Scottish newspaper will be her first step to becoming a reporter. It's an aspiration that
5 separates her from her working-class Catholic parents, who are suspicious of ambition and want everything to continue as it always has. When two small boys are arrested for the murder of a toddler, Paddy believes that the police don't have the whole story, and conducts
10 her own investigation. But this is not simply a murder mystery. Mina produces something special every time and this book – her finest yet – offers a memorable portrait of a touching heroine, along with the dynamics of the workplace and, especially, the family.

B

15 Barbara Vine uses crime as only one element in her books. She is in unusually gentle mood in *The Minotaur*, in which a Swedish woman describes an unsettling experience that happened over 30 years ago, when she was engaged to look after the grown-
20 up son of a bizarre English household. The once grand, now shabby house, is ruled by a tyrannical old woman, whose three unmarried daughters lead separate, dismal lives, moving cautiously around their autistic brother. The narrative is as compelling,
25 but not as dark, as we have come to expect from this distinguished author.

C

The latest addition to Bitter Lemon Press is prize-winning Cuban novelist Leonardo Padura. He does nothing to hinder their mission to publish English
30 translations of the best foreign crime fiction. *Havana Red*, the first book in his Havana quartet, introduces Lieutenant Mario Conde – an eccentric personality with unusual investigative methods. All his skills are called upon when a murder victim turns out to be
35 the son of a prominent diplomat. Padura's powerful writing creates an atmospheric picture of a turbulent city, illuminated by Conde's mocking commentary.

AND OTHER CRIMINALS

D

Jess Walter continues to impress with his new novel *Citizen Vince*, which takes place in the run-up to the
40 1980 US Presidential election. His protagonist, Vince Camden, is a life-long criminal who has avoided another prison sentence by giving evidence against other criminals. He is in witness protection, contentedly managing a doughnut shop, while
45 keeping his hand in with a little credit card fraud, when he discovers that his life is in danger. Vince suddenly realises not only that he enjoys his new life but that, for the first time, it is important to him to vote in an election. His attempts to dodge his assassin
50 and pay off his debts so that he can cast his vote make a splendidly entertaining, thoughtful book.

GREYS

DRINK TIZER THE APPETISER

BLUE RONDO
John Lawton

'Lawton's trick – superbly executed – is to take the threads of history and weave them into his own tapestry.' *The Times*

E

John Lawton's post-Second World War series features the London-based policeman Frederick Troy. Troy is upper-class and his friends and colleagues include
55 both influential figures of society, and faithful (though sometimes less than law-abiding) members of the lower classes. Lawton's plots are tough and Troy spends much of his time in hospital or getting to know various female characters. In *Blue Rondo*, we
60 have reached the 1950s and Troy, now a Chief Superintendent, is investigating a gangland war whilst recovering from yet another injury and … other subplots! Lawton's period atmosphere, illustrated with credible characters, is impeccable and the
65 writing elegantly precise.

F

Harlan Coben has made his intentions clear: he wants to give his protagonist – the good guy – a hard time. And he makes a good job of doing so in *The Innocent*. Everything is going well for Matt Hunter;
70 he has a great job, his wife is expecting their first baby, and they have their ideal American home. But then he finds his life and marriage inexplicably threatened by an unknown man. The enjoyably intricate plot takes several turns, involving a
75 videotape, FBI agents, and even a dead nun, before we are taken on a final twist when the villains and motive are revealed. A book you can't help reading in one go.

Vocabulary

Phrasal verbs: multiple particles

1 Match the phrasal verb with *fall* with the correct meaning in 1–8.
One of the phrasal verbs has two meanings.

fall	a back on	1 fall in love with someone
	b behind	2 be tricked into believing
	c for	3 rely on something when there are no other choices
	d off	4 be very eager to do something
	e through	5 not happen
	f out	6 fail to keep up with
	g over (yourself)	7 decrease
		8 have an argument

2 Complete dialogues 1–8 using the phrasal verbs from 1.

1 A: I'm afraid I've .... with my work this week.
   B: Oh, you'll easily catch up over the weekend.

2 A: Did you manage to find anyone interested in joining the student committee?
   B: Not really – people weren't exactly .... We have to make it sound more appealing.

3 A: What on earth will I do if the new business is not a success?
   B: You can always .... your teaching qualifications – don't worry!

4 A: Did you get that job you wanted with the travel agency?
   B: I didn't. At the last minute the whole thing .... because they filled the vacancy with an internal candidate.

5 A: Did you say James was getting married? I don't believe it.
   B: It's true! He .... for someone he met on holiday and is completely in love.

6 A: Do you get on well with the neighbours?
   B: No. We .... over a year ago and we haven't spoken since.

7 A: I can't believe that you .... that story about Jack being a pilot.
   B: Neither can I – but it seemed plausible at the time.

8 A: Why isn't the football team getting any funding now?
   B: Well, hardly anyone is going to the matches. Attendance has really .... over the last few months.

Grammar

Passives

1 Read the text about an arts academy. Then rewrite each sentence beginning with the words in bold and using the passive form.

BOWLANDS ACADEMY OF ARTS

Someone established **Bowlands Academy of Arts** five years ago. The Department of Education has now officially recognised **the establishment**. The academy offers students **a programme of short, intensive courses**, as well as three-year degree courses. Students can take **a range of examinations** throughout the year. Staff instruct **students** in small groups and they assign every student a personal tutor. Anyone requiring **accommodation in a hall of residence** must book it in advance. Students need to enclose **a deposit** with the enrolment form. The Academy will request **the balance** before the course starts. Students need to inform **the Academy** immediately if they intend to withdraw from their course.

Example
Bowlands Academy of Arts was established five years ago.

2 Complete dialogues 1–7 using the prompts in brackets and a verb from below in the correct form.

▪ steal   service   investigate   confiscate
pierce   dry-clean   test

1 A: I can't read the small print in this document.
   B: Maybe you should go to the optician's and .... (get/eyes) ....
2 A: What's Jill done to herself? She looks different.
   B: It's the earrings. She .... (have/ears) .... last week.
3 A: Look at this stain on my sleeve!
   B: You'll have to .... (get/jacket) ....

4 A: I'd forgotten I had this pair of scissors in my hand-luggage.
   B: They're bound to .... (get) .... by airport security staff.
5 A: The engine won't start.
   B: I don't believe it. We only .... (have/car) .... last week.
6 A: The central locking's broken so I've had to leave the car unlocked.
   B: Let's hope it .... (not/get) ....
7 A: Have you heard anything more about that enormous tax bill you were sent?
   B: Actually, I .... (have/matter) .... by my accountant at this very moment.

3 Rewrite statements a–e using the passive form of the word in italics and beginning with the prompts given.

a There's a *rumour* that the government is going to resign.
   It ....
b Financial experts *predict* interest rates are about to rise.
   Interest rates ....
c Everyone *assumed* the missing gangland leader had been murdered.
   The missing ....
d They *think* the plane crash was due to human error.
   It ....
e People *believe* terrorists are hiding out in the north of the country.
   Terrorists ....

Listening Part 1 Sentence completion

1 What punishments do schoolchildren receive for bad behaviour in your country? Do you think this is an appropriate way to deal with the problem?

2 🎧 Listen to someone talking about 'the cooler room', a punishment used for disruptive schoolchildren at Ninestiles school, and complete sentences 1–9.

THE COOLER ROOM

As many as one 1 .... of the pupils attending Ninestiles school in England gained no qualifications in 1989.

Today is a different story and now the school's 2 .... is outstanding.

'The cooler room' was named after a film called 'The 3 ....'

Disruptive students work in small rooms in the 4 .... unit.

Whilst in the unit, students are provided with .... and 5 ....

A punishment grading of C1 means that students only receive a 6 ....

Students arriving late are given a C3 punishment – 7 .... detention in the cooler room.

As a result of this set of rules, the school has a 8 .... atmosphere.

Chad, a student, chose to 9 .... after being sent to the cooler room.

English in Use Part 2 Open cloze

1 Read the review of the film *Ocean's Twelve*, ignoring the gaps, and find out if the writer enjoyed the film. Why/Why not?

2 Read the text again and complete gaps 1–15.

The film *Ocean's Eleven* (and 0 ...*by*... that, I mean Soderbergh's 2001 hit) had an indefinable quality 1 .... it. But the sequel, unimaginatively titled *Ocean's Twelve*, feels far too much 2 .... the first one.

In the follow-up film, three years 3 .... the first daring robbery, Danny Ocean is found living 4 .... a happy retirement. His wife is waiting at home to celebrate their wedding anniversary, when, 5 .... should arrive, but Terry Benedict. (He's the man from whom Ocean's Eleven, 6 .... the gang has been called, stole 160 million dollars.)

Even 7 .... Benedict has received insurance money for the theft, he now wants the gang to pay it back but 8 .... added interest. 9 .... of them have moved on, but he hunts them down and 10 .... a deal with them – give him nearly 200 million dollars in two weeks, or die.

Faced with 11 .... choice, the gang leave for Amsterdam because it's a place 12 .... they won't be recognised and, with the help of a contact there, they can raise the money. Sadly, this is where *Ocean's Twelve* falls 13 .... and becomes unnecessarily complicated. Perhaps it tries 14 .... hard, maybe it's not trying hard 15 .... , or possibly it's a little of both!

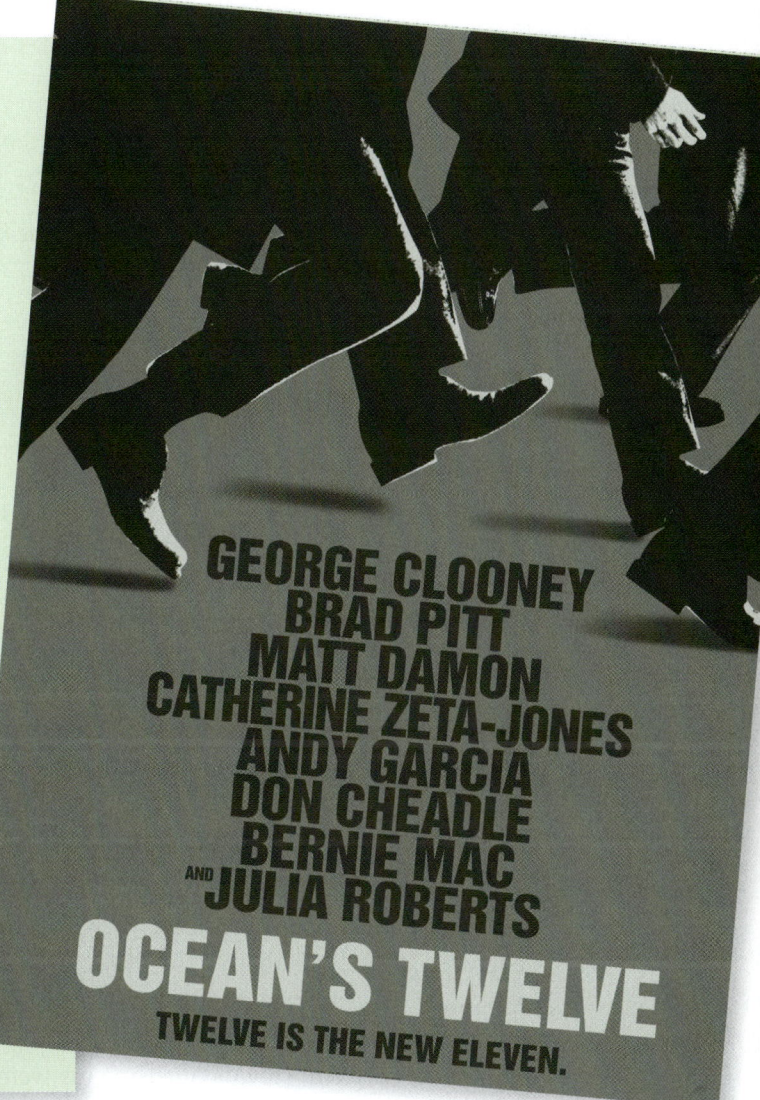

GEORGE CLOONEY
BRAD PITT
MATT DAMON
CATHERINE ZETA-JONES
ANDY GARCIA
DON CHEADLE
BERNIE MAC
AND JULIA ROBERTS

OCEAN'S TWELVE

TWELVE IS THE NEW ELEVEN.

Review Units 7–9

1 Match 1–6 with a–e to make compound adjectives.

1	narrow-	a	handed
2	self-	b	time
3	down	c	hearted
4	first-	d	minded
5	open-	e	made
6	light-		

2 Complete the text about astronomy by putting the words in brackets in a suitable participle form.

1 (peer) .... for years across 1,500 light years of space, scientists now believe they may have found an explanation for creation.
2 (use) .... a sophisticated telescope, scientists have studied hundreds of stars,
3 (identify) .... 27 that behave as the sun did 4.6 billion years ago. The nine planets around the sun were the only ones 4 (know) .... in the whole universe, but 5 (make) .... use of recent observations, astronomers then began to detect other planets. 6 (conclude) .... their research, scientists believe they may have discovered the beginnings of earth-like planets.

3 Complete these sentences using the correct form of *fall* with a suitable particle.

a What's it like to be head-over-heels in love? I've never .... anybody.
b Never .... with your studies. If you do, you'll never catch up.
c When the sale started, crowds of customers were .... to grab a bargain.
d The skiing trip .... in the end, as it proved too complicated to arrange.
e Things haven't been so pleasant here since we .... with the neighbours in the flat above.
f Surely you didn't .... that ridiculous story? It was obvious he was lying!

4 Make nouns from 1–6 using a suitable suffix. Then use them to complete sentences a–f.

1	neighbour	....
2	care	....
3	act	....
4	employ	....
5	friend	....
6	child	....

a Sally won .... of the month at her office!
b I think socialising and making new .... are the most enjoyable parts of my life.
c I spent my .... in Scotland; it was an amazing place to grow up.
d Nicole Kidman is my favourite .... I adore all her films.
e This .... is very exclusive; it's an extremely affluent area.
f He is unbelievably .... with his work and continuously makes mistakes.

5 Correct the mistakes in the passive form in sentences a–g.

a The package was arrived safely and on schedule this morning.
b Tonight's recital is been given by a well-known pianist.
c Exhibit 451 is being thought to have been painted by Picasso.
d This violin is to be considered the best example of a period instrument of this kind.
e I can't stand having made to do what I consider to be a waste of time.
f A collection of priceless gold coins has being discovered in a castle on the south coast.
g According to the police, this building could have abandoned for some time.

6 Write the correct phrasal verb with *off* or *in* for definitions a–g.

a try to understand the meaning   t...............
b try to impress people   s...............
c request to come and help   c...............
d begin to be successful   t...............
e introduce   b...............
f interrupt   c...............
g succeed against expectations   b...............

7 Add the correct negative prefix to adjectives 1–8, then match them with synonyms a–h.

1	........tolerable	a	inaccessible
2	........reversible	b	inhospitable
3	........stable	c	indistinguishable
4	........sensitive	d	insecure
5	........sociable	e	incalculable
6	........penetrable	f	unbearable
7	........perceptible	g	uncaring
8	........measurable	h	unchangeable

8 Underline the correct conditional form in sentences a–g.

a If I *would have/had* enough free time, I would do voluntary work.
b If she *asks/had asked* me, I'll consider helping out at the festival.
c If they *had left/leave* home earlier, they would not have missed the train.
d If students *read/would read* English newspapers, it helps improve their vocabulary.
e If you *see/had seen* Ben this morning, remind him to pick up those tickets.
f If I *went/had visited* Australia, I might have emigrated permanently.
g If the restaurant *was/wasn't* so expensive, we could go there for our anniversary.

9 Complete gaps a–i in the table with the correct form of the words given.

	noun – thing	noun – person
a	politics	....
b	music	....

	noun – thing	adjective
c	....	content
d	anxiety	....
e	clarity	....
f	....	secret
g	diplomacy	....
h	....	authentic
i	democracy	....

Buying and selling

Reading Part 2 Gapped text

1 Quickly read the article about the textile industry in China. What facts or figures do you find suprising?

2 Read the article again and match paragraphs A–G with gaps 1–6. There is one extra paragraph.

dressing for **success**

The next time you get dressed, cast your mind eastwards towards Qiaotou. For no matter whether you are wearing bell-bottomed jeans, a pencil skirt or tailored trousers, the chances are that the button or zip comes from this dusty, dirty town. Located in the middle of nowhere, this is the sort of place you might drive through without noticing. It is too small to be marked on most western maps of China, too insignificant to merit a mention in newspapers, and barely known outside the local area. But in just twenty-five years, this humble community has destroyed most of its international rivals to become the undisputed global capital of buttons and zips.

1 ....

The commercial revolution here is on a scale and at a pace that exceeds anything experienced before. The first small workshop was established in 1980 by three brothers who picked their first buttons off the street. Now the town's 700 family-run factories churn out 15 billion buttons and 200 million metres of zips a year. The low-investment, labour-intensive industry was ideal for this remote community. And it could not have timed its rise better. Qiaotou began popping buttons just as

China started dressing up. Out went the Mao suits, and in came chic western clothes. So this is the place to head for if you're looking for a button of exactly the right shape, size and material, to adorn those new fashions hanging in your wardrobe.

2 ....

Such mind-boggling export statistics, until recently, were used as evidence of the Chinese miracle. Now, however, the global domination of manufacturing towns such as this is increasingly being discussed in very different terms: as a sign of a threat to other manufacturing countries. After the Cultural Revolution, the world cheered on the market-oriented reforms. Growth of more than 9% a year for more than two decades has lifted hundreds of millions out of poverty. Consumers across the globe have benefited from the cheap goods made by factory workers in Qiaotou and elsewhere.

3 ....

But Chinese businessmen are unfazed by this action. 'Even if we lose a few customers in the short term, they will have to come back,' says the president of the Great Wall Zipper group. 'There is almost nowhere else in the world that makes zips.'

4 ....

Take, for instance, Yiwu. If China is the workshop of the world, Yiwu is its showroom. Selling everything from engine parts to hair clips and costume jewellery, this town's market has grown from a few dozen street stalls ten years ago to become the world's biggest commodity trading centre.

5 ....

And it is hard to imagine that this worldwide monopoly will end any time soon; Lanswe, the biggest sock manufacturer in the world, spins out two million socks a day. Within two years the company plans to triple its workforce to 15,000 and increase output to five million socks a day. Textile quotas or no textile quotas, half of them are destined for export.

6 ....

The view from China is that foreign countries say they want China to develop, but when it does, they become nervous. China is changing. The countryside is changing and change is a cause for hope. But China needs to be given time to make sure its miracle does not sour.

A

And buyers do indeed come here from all over the world. Attracted by prices of less than a penny a zip and the decent quality, international retail outlets and fashion houses are increasingly purchasing from Qiaotou. The local chamber of commerce estimates that three out of every five buttons in the world are made in the town, which boasts 1,300 button shops selling 1,400 varieties of buttons. It ships more than two million zips a day, making it the biggest winner of China's 80% share of the international zip market.

B

Talk of unfair currency manipulation and the need for trade quotas is nothing new. The domination of the world markets for cars and electronics in the 1980s led to a fierce trade dispute and pressure for appreciation of the yen. When this eventually did happen, the flood of money into the country inflated an enormous speculative bubble in the early 90s.

C

And what was once a modest farming village is now a manufacturing powerhouse – a microcosm of what has happened to the entire Chinese economy in the last few decades. It is a familiar story: paddy fields have been cleared for factories and peasants have become industrialists. The river, which used to be a clean source for irrigation, is now a heavily polluted outlet for brightly coloured plastic waste.

D

The same confidence prevails throughout the south coastal provinces. With endless streets of giant factories and company dormitories, the most developed areas are modern-day equivalents of Western cities at the peak of the Industrial Revolution. The many small towns, some not even on maps, have become world-beaters by focusing on labour-intensive niches.

E

The company's president says he can understand why countries want to restrict this growth and impose certain limits, even though it might hurt his business. 'Even if the yuan gets stronger, rich countries will still import socks because they cannot make them cheaply enough themselves.' He believes that, in the long run, change must come through market forces rather than export quotas and currency manipulation. 'If rich nations really want to compete with China, they need to make us richer. That's the best way to make prices rise here.'

F

After a decade of towns like this one growing almost unnoticed, the world has suddenly realised just how powerful they have become. Thanks to globalisation, the clothes of the world are being zipped and buttoned up by deft-fingered migrant workers, our teeth are being brushed with bristles from Huang Zi, and our toes are being kept warm by the products of Yiwu.

G

But recently, the rejoicing has been replaced by warnings. A flood of Chinese goods has swept into European and American markets, threatening jobs and alarming governments. One administration responded by setting a limit on shipments of jackets, trousers and shirts. Others have taken a less aggressive line, by setting quotas to protect their clothing industries from the competition in China.

Vocabulary

Money

1 Match the words in 1–4 with definitions a or b.

1 fee / fare
   a money paid to travel by public transport
   b money paid for professional advice or services

2 bill / receipt
   a a piece of paper showing how much you owe for goods and services
   b a piece of paper showing that goods or services have been paid for

3 salary / wage
   a the annual amount of money paid to an employee
   b the daily or weekly amount of money paid to an employee

4 cash / change
   a a small amount of money, normally coins
   b money in the form of coins or notes, rather than a cheque or credit card

2 Complete sentences a–d with words from 1.

a .... for manual work are still way behind those of skilled workers.
b Tuition .... are one of many issues facing students today.
c Have you got some .... to leave a tip for the waiter?
d Make sure that you get a .... when you pay for the goods.

Word formation (3)

3 Underline the correct ending for the verbs a–i.

a fals...   ate/en/ify
b strength...   ate/en/ify
c activ...   ate/en/ify
d rect...   ate/en/ify
e broad...   ate/en/ify
f typ...   ate/en/ify
g altern...   ate/en/ify
h demonstr...   ate/en/ify
i sadd...   ate/en/ify

4 Use one of the verbs from 3 in the correct form to complete these sentences.

a Opposition to our plans .... and increased our determination to put them into action.
b To be fluent in another language, you should .... the vocabulary you learn by using it as often as possible.
c It later became apparent that the documentation had been .... and we had all been misled.
d The mood of the waiting crowd .... between boredom and excitement.
e If you can find a way to .... the situation, then no-one will know about your mistakes!
f We were all .... to hear about the loss of your grandfather and send our sympathy.
g After working in the same city for ten years, I decided to .... my horizons and travel the world.

Grammar Mixed conditionals

1 Make conditional sentences from the boxes below. There may be more than one possibility.

a Permission for the event will not be given		it's an emergency.
b What you may have done in the past is not important	unless	you are honest with me now.
	provided	I wanted you to be involved in it?
c I never use my mobile phone	as long as	he'd been forced to.
d Would you agree to the scheme	supposing	all safety regulations are complied with.
e Jim would never have changed his job		

2 Choose the correct option, a or b, to complete sentences 1–7.

1 I wish I .... afford to upgrade my computer system.
   a would be able to   b could

2 My brother wishes he .... the firm he is currently working for.
   a didn't join   b hadn't joined

3 Don't you wish you .... speak more languages fluently?
   a could   b would

4 If only my boss .... me to work all day long.
   a haven't expected   b didn't expect

5 Do you ever wish you .... to go somewhere else on holiday?
   a had chosen   b chose

6 If only people .... keep interrupting me in mid-sentence!
   a won't   b wouldn't

7 I wish I .... to your advice.
   a wouldn't listen   b hadn't listened

Grammar Extra Determiners

3 Circle the correct determiner to complete sentences a–j.

a *The whole/All the* idea of raising money to keep run-down museums open seems pointless.
b There is *not many/hardly any* good news in the media these days.
c The question of whether we can actually help developing countries by giving aid is a difficult *one/other*.
d *None/Neither* of the advice that Charlotte offered was useful to me.
e *Every/Each* of the paintings on loan for the exhibition has been insured against damage.
f Unfortunately, due to my family commitments, I have *a little/little* time to myself these days.
g *Loads/Several* of people came to the opening of the Italian restaurant.
h Some traffic restrictions do prevent accidents, whereas *others/another* merely cause traffic jams.
i Fortunately, *a few/few* people managed to make it to work yesterday, despite the atrocious weather conditions.
j The *most/whole* we can do is hope they don't notice our mistakes.

Listening Part 3 Multiple choice

1 What problems or consequences do you think 'music piracy' (illegally obtaining music) may cause?

2 🎧 Listen to an interview with a journalist, Sam Broadbent, who is talking about music piracy, and choose the correct answers for 1–6.

1 According to Sam, the issue of music piracy is complicated because
   A too many private individuals are being taken to court.
   B it's unclear who should actually be prosecuted.
   C it's difficult to prevent people buying the necessary software.
   D the entertainment industry is making downloading too desirable.

2 What happened in one legal case in 1984?
   A The use of video recorders was banned in certain places.
   B The entertainment industry successfully sued a video manufacturer.
   C It was decided that the main purpose of video recording was not illegal.
   D A video manufacturer was found guilty of making illegal copies of films.

3 Sam says the current legal case
   A concentrates on the many people losing their income.
   B doesn't question how the products are used.
   C is targeting the firms that enable people to download illegally.
   D suggests the banning of illegal products.

4 What is Sam's greatest fear?
   A People will stop worrying about whether downloading is right or wrong.
   B The development of downloading technology will be slowed.
   C People in the entertainment industry will no longer be active.
   D Manufacturers of new technology will constantly be involved in lawsuits.

5 According to Sam, many members of the public he has talked to feel that
   A copyright laws should be further tightened.
   B the products they buy could be less expensive.
   C the entertainment industry is losing out financially.
   D distribution costs should be passed on to the manufacturers.

6 In Sam's opinion, films should be released
   A much more quickly on DVD.
   B in Europe before being released in the USA.
   C on the Internet and at the cinema at the same time.
   D in cinemas all over the world simultaneously.

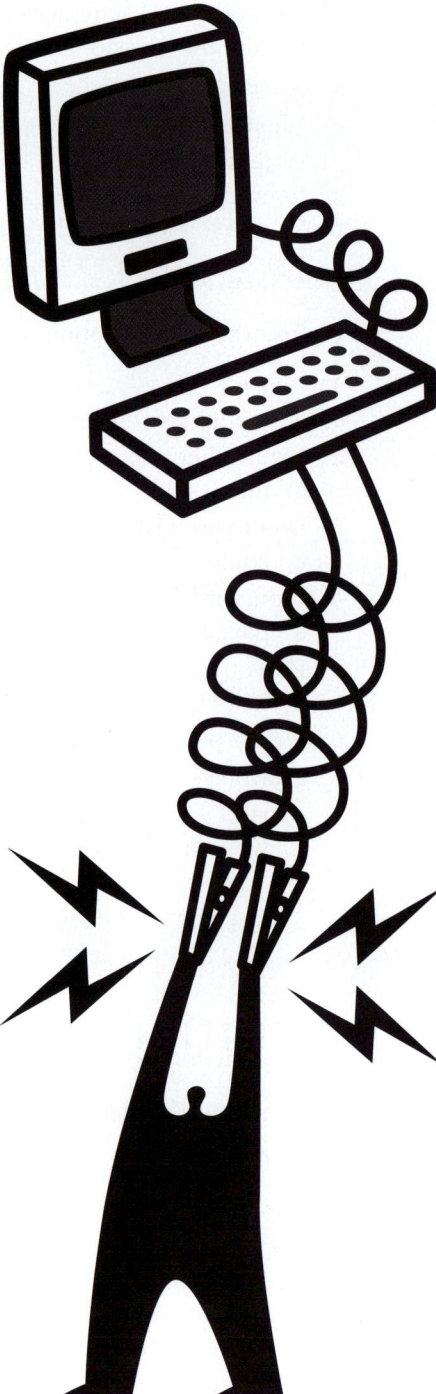

English in Use

Part 3 Error correction

1 Read the article about 'Freecycle' and find out what it is and how it started.

2 Read the article again and find the lines which have an unnecessary word.

Giving it away

Examples: 0 ✓
            00 *are*

0	Resisting the temptation to buy is hard, be it a new outfit, gadget or
00	a little treat. Now guilty shoppers are keen to get rid of unwanted
01	purchases have a new option – simply give it away online. As if the name
02	suggests, which everything advertised on Freecycle must be free – whether
03	it's unwanted CDs, old jeans or even a few of hours' help in the garden. Anyone
04	interested in simply replies by email and the deal goes ahead. Freecycle
05	is just one website which is playing an extremely valuable part in the
06	reducing the amount of rubbish be sent to landfill sites by encouraging a
07	more efficient form of recycling – simply giving things to people who want
08	them. The site is the creation of Deron Beal, an environmentalist from
09	Arizona, who was started it as a list on the Internet. Today, it resembles
10	like a cross between an Internet auction house and a global chain of charity
11	shops. Mr Beal says his chief aim is to have cut waste and help the
12	environment. 'I live in a beautiful desert area and, in the middle of it, you've
13	got to this hideous landfill, overflowing with perfectly good, reusable stuff,'
14	Mr Beal recently told reporters. The Freecycle network now has 1.2 million
15	members in 2,700 centres worldwide. So if you want a sofa, and the
16	seller lives nearby, it can be picked up on rather than posted!

Entertainment or art?

Reading Part 3 Multiple choice

1 **Read the article about the artist Giancarlo Neri and find out**

a   the title of his piece of work.
b   where the artist rented his first studio.
c   who Augusto Nunzi was.

2 **Read the article again and choose the best answer (A, B, C or D) to questions 1–6.**

1   What do we learn initially about this example of Neri's art?
   A   It was designed for people exercising their dogs.
   B   The inspiration for it came when he was in Italy.
   C   Its creation has been a rather slow process.
   D   It was originally created for a different site.

2   Neri believes that his piece of art
   A   is best viewed from a particular bench in the park.
   B   would have been equally effective in several locations.
   C   reflects the history and culture of its location.
   D   has been greatly admired by local inhabitants.

3   What happens whenever Neri tries to install his works of art?
   A   He gets upset when people object to his ideas.
   B   He comes up against opposition from local artists.
   C   He refuses to talk to people who disapprove of the idea.
   D   He makes sure he complies with local rules and regulations.

4   What inspired Neri's first artistic creation?
   A   the football stadium in Naples
   B   what he could see from his New York studio
   C   his football career with a New York team
   D   a visit to a local prison

5   It appears as if Neri's creation 'The Writer'
   A   is made from an unusual variety of hazelwood.
   B   was based on a design by a local ironmonger.
   C   had to be constructed in a field because of its size.
   D   surprised even its creator when completed.

6   How does Neri sum up his feelings about art?
   A   People fail to appreciate the most beautiful art of all.
   B   Artists are capable of far more than they realise.
   C   Only art can portray the real beauty of our surroundings.
   D   True art is only represented in our memories.

suffering for his art

Endless nuts and bolts have been screwed into place. Like a giant piece of flat pack furniture, a table and chair has been assembled on the rolling slopes of Parliament Hill in London by a team of engineers directed by Italian artist Giancarlo Neri. It towers skywards and makes dog walkers look Lilliputian in size. Neri, fifty, has been planning this moment for an incredible four years; from when he first laid eyes on Parliament Hill, the Neopolitan knew he had found the perfect spot for 'The Writer'. And this giant piece of public art has instantly become a new landmark.

The site was chosen when Neri spoke to a friend who lives nearby. He described the project he was working on and she said three places would suit: Primrose Hill, Richmond, and the Heath. As soon as he saw Primrose Hill, his mind was made up. 'I sat on a bench and looked across the fields. I just knew it was the right place,' he says. However he doesn't suggest viewers should find that particular bench which told him he had found the right place. 'Stand back and admire it – find your own spot.' Neri believes the theme of the sculpture fitted in with the area, because 'it is a statement on the loneliness of art. When you read a book, you rarely think of the person behind it, sitting alone at their table for years. This place has inspired hundreds of writers and I think that is why it was accepted, because there was a heritage intertwined with literature.'

But it nearly didn't happen. As with all of Neri's art (he has been doing similar pieces for twenty-four years) he has had to overcome a tangle of bureaucracy to make his vision become reality. He says, 'The enemy of my work is bureaucracy. Obtaining permits takes more time and trouble than anything else.' He has previously battled with authorities when trying to install a Trojan Horse in Naples Harbour and giant footballs installed from bridges in New York. Although he did find that the local Council and the Corporation of London were alive to the idea. 'I tried talking to the committee so they could see what I was about,' he remembers. 'One member objected at first, but then he came to see me and told me how impressive he finds it.' Others refused to even talk to him. But he believes the complaints were from a small minority. 'I'm not hurt by negative reactions. Should people who do not want to see it here have the final say over whether it will go up? I don't know. I went through the proper avenues and contacted the right people; I haven't put it up in the middle of the night.'

Neri was born in Naples in 1955, a stone's throw from the San Paolo football stadium, home of Napoli FC. And football was one of his first loves; he played professionally with the New York Apollo team in the 1970s. He later turned his back on football to go to art school and his first installation came about because of the garret he was living in. He had a small studio in Manhattan, by Union Square – 'it was the size of a prison cell' – to paint in. Whilst the views were great, it was too small to hang work. So he had an idea. 'I was looking out of the window, and saw these marvellous rooftops. I thought: I should hang my art there – that way, my window can become a work of art.' He got his neighbour's permission and started making canvases on the facades facing his studio. It was the start of a career that has seen him take his work to outdoor spaces across the world.

'The Writer' was created and built in Italy. After coming up with the concept Neri had to find an ironmonger able to put the plans into action. He searched for the right foundry, and discovered it in an unusual place. On the outskirts of Rome lie fields of hazelnut trees and driving through them one day, he came across Augusto Nunzi's workshop, which normally makes parts for hazelnut-harvesting equipment. He built the chair and table in his yard following Neri's designs and the artist clearly remembers driving back weeks after the designs had been handed over, 'It had a 'wow' factor. Even though I knew how big it was going to be, I didn't realise how impressive it would look. I was taken aback, and I hope people walking here will feel the same.'

He is far from being troubled by the transient nature of his art and explains that 'because they are temporary, it means I can get away with doing things I otherwise would not be able to. Sometimes you wonder if it is worth the effort. But that is part of it; it's a snap shot. Hopefully it will stay in the memories of people who have seen it.' One of the points of his philosophy is that art is all around us and is rarely noticed. Standing at the foot of Parliament Hill and looking at the willow trees that dot the banks of the wildfowl pond, he agrees it would make a great painting. But he believes the true beauty of the scene could never really be captured by the human eye and hand. 'It's as beautiful as it can be; no reproduction can do a view like that justice. It's like the sea and the moon – amazing, natural art.' ●

Vocabulary

Three-part phrasal verbs

1 Make two three-part phrasal verbs from each of the boxes below.

1	put	down	with
		up	to
2	get	down	with
	come	away	
3	drop	in	of
		out	on

2 Use the phrasal verbs from 1 to replace the words in italics in a–f.

a We don't *tolerate* that kind of behaviour in this school.

b Not many people went to the exhibition. I *think this is because of* the location – it's really hard to find that gallery.

c In winter many elderly people *become ill with* the 'flu.

d How did Bob manage to *go unpunished for* forgetting his wedding anniversary?

e Almost half of the students *chose to stop going to* the debating society meetings.

f I'm just going to *quickly visit* Jill for a coffee – do you want to come along?

3 Choose the correct verb in sentences a–h to make three-part phrasal verbs.

a We should *look/take/go* up to the older generation – they have so much wisdom.

b I'm afraid the job didn't *pull/live/move* up to my expectations so I decided to hand in my notice.

c Dad will just have to *look/face/sit* up to the fact that he's not as young as he used to be.

d The only way to deal with bullies is either to run away or *stand/push/call* up to them.

e No one *saw/felt/went* up to going to the concert so we stayed at home instead.

f Thanks for the lovely lunch. It's great to see you, but I'm afraid I've got to *get/take/move* back to work. Bye!

g There was so much to do in the week *going/leading/walking* up to the holiday, that we were exhausted when we finally got on the plane.

h Why don't you *start/wake/jump* up to the fact that you will never pass your exams, if you go out all the time?

4 Match phrasal verbs from 3 with meanings 1–8.

1 respect
2 want to do something
3 return
4 confront someone
5 approach or prepare for something
6 accept that something is true
7 be as good as expected
8 appreciate a situation

Grammar

Comparatives and superlatives

1 Correct the mistakes with comparatives and superlatives in sentences a–f.

a Have you read his latest novel? It's so boring and just as all the others.

b Sarah hated travelling by coach. In her opinion, it was by far the worse choice. The train was simply the best option.

c She's a lot as her sister. They're both extremely creative and have fiery tempers.

d The more time I spend travelling, the little I want to settle down in one place.

e Why don't we go to the modern art gallery on Thornton Street? It's far interesting than the other one.

f I've never had such a boring holiday. It was not near as good as I thought it would be.

2 Complete sentences a–h using the words below.

■ just   no more   nothing   nowhere   great
bit   nearly   slightly

a Booking online is only .... cheaper than booking by phone.

b According to the airlines, air travel is .... as safe as any other from of transport.

c Season tickets aren't .... as expensive as those bought on a daily basis.

d Buying decent quality sportswear is .... expensive than buying clothes with a designer label.

e Unfortunately, the band's latest album is .... near as good as their previous one.

f Learning to play the piano is .... like as difficult as learning to play the violin.

g If you worked a .... harder, you might actually achieve your objectives.

h Travelling alone is a .... deal more exciting than travelling in a group.

3 Choose four of the expressions in 2 and use them in sentences to compare
• watching DVDs or going to the cinema
• listening to CDs and going to a concert
• modern art and Renaissance art

Grammar Extra

so and *such*

4 Complete sentences a–g using *so* or *such*.

a Fresh vegetables, ... as cauliflowers and aubergines, are available at the market.

b The measures have been introduced .... that safety standards can be improved.

c We consider ourselves fortunate to have .... friendly neighbours.

d Housing is expensive in the capital and .... is the cost of parking.

e 'Is Mike here yet?' 'Yes, I think ....'

f It was .... a complicated form that no one could understand how to fill it in.

g Fifty or .... people attended the lecture.

5 Match the examples of *so* and *such* in 4 with uses 1–6 below.

1 to give an example
2 to indicate that something is not exact
3 to say that something else is true
4 to emphasise
5 to offer an explanation
6 to avoid repeating a phrase

Listening

Part 2 Sentence completion

1 Which of the following do you think is necessary to show that you appreciate modern art?

- having a thorough knowledge of art
- obtaining a qualification in art
- creating your own works of art
- behaving in a certain manner at galleries
- owning works by famous artists

2 🎧 Listen to an expert giving some advice on art appreciation and complete sentences 1–8.

how to appreciate modern art

Remember that modern art began around the year .... 1.

The aim of modern art was to rebel against .... 2.

It is essential to .... 3 at a gallery.

You need to wear .... 4 during your visit.

Never stand where the .... 5 interfere with your appreciation of a painting.

Remember that .... 6 is taken extremely seriously in galleries.

You can actually get a better view by .... 7 and using binoculars.

Make sure you only stop to look at .... 8 works of art.

English in Use

1 Read the article about a portable media centre and find out what the writer thinks are its weaknesses.

2 Choose the best phrase (A–J) to complete the gaps in the article. There are three extra phrases.

A should you find yourself temporarily short of funds
B when you choose a model that downloads from websites
C if you're simply confused by technology
D unless you choose a model with lots of space for memory
E when you're a member of the computer generation
F when you want to keep abreast of current events
G if you are going to be watching a lot of films
H if you want all your entertainment and pictures in one place
I if you've always loved playing with computers
J *if you are the kind of person who is always on the move*

ENTERTAINMENT WHILE YOU TRAVEL

Complete entertainment is now available to travellers at the press of a button. This new games console that is also a 'portable media centre' will provide you with hours of amusement wherever you happen to be – perfect 0 ...J... . These gadgets can hold hundreds of films, thousands of songs and all your favourite photos so 1 .... , this is definitely the gadget for you.

Some models are very similar to computers in that they contain a hard drive and even a huge memory, which is fine 2 .... who has been brought up on such gadgets. But what if you're not part of this age group or 3 .... ? Well, in that case, you may find them a bit confusing at first.

Looking at the consoles, you may be surprised at how small the screens are. And 4 .... , you need to make sure that the screen is large enough to appreciate them.

And be warned that having lots of films may mean having less music or fewer photos – 5 .... One final thing to remember is that 6 .... , you will need a connection to the Internet which could prove to be frustratingly slow. So weigh up all your options carefully before making your purchase.

A changing world

Reading Parts 1 and 4 Multiple matching

1 Read the article about how to be environmentally friendly. Which summary of the writer's comments (a–c) is the most accurate?

a   There are numerous ways to help the planet.
b   It is pointless to try to follow schemes and ideas.
c   We should be aware of unexpected consequences of our actions.

2 Read the article again and decide in which paragraph (A–E) the following are mentioned.

a controversial pastime that raises considerable money	1 …	
an action which creates a different weather pattern	2 …	
an undesirable result of unnecessary global transportation	3 …	4 …
inadequate research into harmful substances	5 …	
a continual change in what is required or needed	6 …	
people at the greatest risk from factors beyond their control	7 …	
a far-reaching change in official attitude	8 …	
a benefit for those the scheme was not originally intended for	9 …	10 …
the bringing of a source of energy to remote areas	11 …	
a failure to adapt in order to meet increasing demands	12 …	

But will it save the planet?

A Fair trade

Farmers in developing countries are some of the most vulnerable people on earth, prey to world commodity markets, middle men and the weather. So-called 'fair-trade' arrangements guarantee co-operative groups a
5 price above the world market and a bonus on top. The growing fair-trade market has distributed hundreds of millions of pounds to more than 50 million people worldwide. But critics say that fair trade will never lift a country out of poverty; indeed, it may keep it there,
10 because the money generated from sales goes almost in its entirety to rich countries which promote the products. As a simple guide, only about 5% of the sale price of a fair-trade chocolate bar may actually go to the poor country.

B Organic food

15 For food to be organic it must be free of added chemicals, both in the growing of the food and in the killing of the pests that might damage the crop. In a world where many manufactured chemicals have never been properly tested for safety, this is a very big selling
20 point. Parents are thus prepared to pay a premium for organic food, especially when chemicals suspected of causing a variety of problems have been found, albeit in tiny quantities, in most children's blood. The problem is that many farmers have not switched to
25 organic in sufficient numbers to satisfy this growing market. As a result, supermarkets are often forced to fly vegetables they can label 'organic' halfway round the world, at a great cost to the planet in extra greenhouse gases. Environmentalists are now urging shoppers to
30 buy locally produced vegetables, even if they are not organic and have been sprayed with pesticides.

C Recycling

A great shift has taken place in the way we think about rubbish. Where once we were happy to bury it in landfills or dump it at sea, we are now being urged by
35 national and local governments to recycle it and think of waste as a resource. The wheelie-bin culture is being replaced by a series of kerbside collections for paper, metals, plastic, bottles, clothes and compost. The idea is to cut landfill as well as saving the planet. It is, however,
40 having some unexpected consequences. Most of Britain's plastic and paper is now being sent for recycling in China or India, which creates more greenhouse gases just to get it there, plus workers then have to separate it. Meanwhile, some paper and bottles carefully sorted out
45 by householders end up being dumped in landfills after all, because the demand for recycled materials constantly fluctuates.

D Being carbon neutral

If you want to make yourself feel better about the planet, there are lots of ways for you to ease your
50 conscience by becoming 'carbon neutral'. One of the most appealing methods is to pay for someone to plant trees, preferably creating or regenerating new forests. The theory is that trees grow by absorbing carbon dioxide and giving out oxygen, storing the
55 carbon in their trunks. But woods and forests create their own mini-climate, which collects and stores water and creates rainclouds. Added to this, there is the potential problem that planting trees often releases carbon stored in the soil – and what happens if the
60 forests catch fire, or are chopped down and harvested for timber? Another and perhaps better solution might be to invest in small-scale hydro-electric schemes, so that people who live in the Himalayas, for example, and currently do not have electricity, can develop a
65 21st century lifestyle without polluting the planet.

E Eco-tourism

The idea of 'green' tourism is to persuade local people not to chop down forests, shoot elephants or wipe out tigers, but to preserve them so rich tourists visit and peer at the wildlife through binoculars. Unfortunately,
70 the best money is made from reintroducing animals for trophy hunting by the very rich – an idea which does not always meet with approval and has caused much debate. While tourists may help sustain some national parks, they often create as many problems as they solve.
75 One is that they tend to demand all mod cons in their hotels, such as a great deal of water for showers; a luxury sometimes not available for locals. Eco-tourism, when properly managed, can offer the locals and the animals a brighter future. Sometimes, though, the only
80 winners are a few business people who own hotels.

Vocabulary

Meanings of *set*

1 Choose the correct meaning (A–C) of the verb *set* in 1–8.

1 Diana's birthday present was a ruby *set* in a gold ring.
   A organised   B positioned   C marked

2 A deadline for the assignment has not yet been *set*.
   A decided   B regulated   C concluded

3 All questions for the quiz are *set* by experts in their field.
   A studied   B published   C written

4 Leave twenty-four hours for the glue to *set*.
   A harden   B soften   C widen

5 Howard's latest film is *set* in an indeterminate time in the future.
   A comes about   B goes on   C takes place

6 The waitress *set* the dining tables using the best cutlery and crockery.
   A prepared   B placed   C piled

7 Some schools *set* extremely high standards for their students.
   A insert   B enforce   C present

8 Our teacher's friendly manner always *set* the tone for her classes.
   A established   B arranged   C insisted

2 Match phrases a–e with 1–5, inserting the verb *set* in the correct form.

a The writer explained that he …
b To make sure the jelly …
c Since its creation five years ago, the school …
d The university always …
e Unfortunately the date for the reunion …

1 high standards for others to aspire to.
2 early enough to obtain the preferred venue.
3 all applicants an intelligence test.
4 you need to put it in a cool place.
5 his latest novel in France because he had lived there as a child.

Words with similar meanings (3)

3 Complete sentences a and b with the correct form of the words in 1–3.

1 refuse / decline
   a We have to .... your invitation to the opening as we have a prior engagement.
   b Paul .... to admit that he had been the one to cause the accident.

2 refute / reject
   a Despite several job offers, Julia .... them and went back to university.
   b Many people have tried to .... the scientist's theories with opposing evidence.

3 deny / disallow
   a The accused .... being anywhere near the scene of the crime.
   b There were numerous objections when the goal was ....

4 Use the correct form of the verbs below to replace the words in italics in sentences a–e.

   assure   ensure   insure   secure   ascertain

a Could passengers please *make sure* they have all their belongings with them before leaving the aircraft?
b All doors and windows must be *locked* when the building is vacated.
c I was *told it was true* that the tickets would be delivered on Monday.
d We strongly advise customers to *take out a policy protecting* their possessions when travelling.
e The purpose of this form is to *discover* whether you are eligible for the loan you have requested.

Grammar

Emphasis

1 Match a–g with 1–7 to make complete sentences.

a In no way …
b Only when …
c Little …
d Scarcely …
e No sooner …
f Under no circumstances …
g Nowhere …

1 had the boat left the quay than a storm blew up.
2 we opened the front door did we realise that we had been burgled.
3 had the lead marathon runner reached the finishing line when she collapsed.
4 is this newspaper report a true representation of what actually happened.
5 in the city do staff treat you better than in this hotel.
6 did William suspect what lay in store for him.
7 will I ever speak to him again.

Grammar Extra

too and *enough*

2 Rewrite these sentences using the words in brackets.

Example

The sea isn't warm enough for us to go swimming. (too).
The sea is too cold for us to go swimming.

a Pat is too short to be a professional dancer.
(enough) ....
b There aren't enough people using public transport nowadays.
(far too) ....
c The training course is too expensive for most people to consider enrolling.
(enough) ....
d I'm not old enough to drive.
(too) ....
e He spoke too quickly for me to hear what he said.
(enough) ....

3 Insert *too* or *enough* in the correct place in sentences a–h.

a If the tea is not hot, I can make you another cup.
b I'm young to vote in an election this year, but next year I'll be able to.
c There's much poverty in the world today.
d Is there time to look at the shops before we check in?
e Didn't you find that documentary far complicated?
f I'm afraid you are just not studying hard this term.
g Have you really got experience to apply for the job?
h Please speak clearly for everyone to hear you.

Listening Part 4 Multiple matching

1 What are the main environmental concerns in your country?

2 🎧 Listen to five people talking environmental issues and do the exam task below.

For 1–5, choose from A–H what the people would like governments to do.

A take action now without having to explain their decisions

B provide more funding for thorough scientific studies

C make sure the information they base decisions on is reliable

D pass laws preventing people from harming the environment

E make sure everyone knows the consequences of international travel

F give more individual responsibilities to specific nations

G help poorer nations become more environmentally friendly

H try to get rid of all threats to the environment

Speaker 1 ☐ 1

Speaker 2 ☐ 2

Speaker 3 ☐ 3

Speaker 4 ☐ 4

Speaker 5 ☐ 5

For 6–10, choose from A–H why the people would like governments to do these things.

A to encourage more students to consider science as a career

B to highlight the harm caused by people's ways of living

C to try to limit the amount of climate change already taking place

D to utilise all available natural resources on the planet

E to find answers to questions we cannot answer at the moment

F to prevent developing nations making mistakes made by other nations

G to avoid making decisions which could have damaging financial results

H to increase the production of cheap types of fuel

Speaker 1 ☐ 6

Speaker 2 ☐ 7

Speaker 3 ☐ 8

Speaker 4 ☐ 9

Speaker 5 ☐ 10

English in Use

1 Read the memo below. What problem does the supermarket want to help with and how does it intend to do this?

2 Read the leaflet below, then use the information in the memo to complete gaps 1–12. Remember to use no more than two words in each gap.

MEMO

Barbara

Could you put together a leaflet for customers explaining why we've decided to stop giving out plastic bags in our supermarket? We should mention the following:

On average everyone takes home 150 plastic bags every year – across the whole world that adds up to one million a minute.

After they've been thrown away, the wind can blow them off landfill sites to create litter everyone can see, and they can hang around in the environment for several years. In Bangladesh, the Buriganga river was almost completely blocked with bags and most people think it was the bags blocking the drains that caused the terrible floods there in 1988 and 1998.

Apart from that they are particularly dangerous to wildlife. Increasingly often, people come across dead turtles and whales washed up on beaches with plastic bags in their stomachs. In the water, a carrier bag looks almost exactly like a jellyfish to them.

You could finish by saying that we hope the customers will understand our reasons, and that they'll join us in trying to do away with plastic bags.

WHY WE'VE SAID 'NO' TO PLASTIC BAGS

Did you know that on average we take home 150 plastic bags 1 .... ? In other words a 2 .... figure of one million every minute.

Once they've been 3 .... of, they can be blown from landfill sites to produce highly 4 .... litter which can remain in the environment for 5 .... of years.

Plastic bags almost dammed the Buriganga river in Bangladesh, and they are widely held 6 .... causing devastating floods there on two occasions.

They also pose a particular 7 .... to wildlife. More and more 8 .... , dead turtles and whales 9 .... washed up on beaches after swallowing plastic bags. To marine life, a plastic bag 10 .... a jellyfish.

We hope these examples 11 .... our decision, and that you will give us 12 .... in making the plastic bag a thing of the past.

Review Units 10–12

1 Complete the endings of verbs a–i.

a   activ...............
b   typ...............
c   sadd...............
d   altern...............
e   strength...............
f   rect...............
g   fals...............
h   demonstr...............
i   broad...............

2 Write two comparative sentences for each pair of sentences in a–e. Use the words in brackets.
Example
Brass is cheap. Gold is expensive. (nowhere near)
Brass is nowhere near as expensive as gold. Gold is nowhere near as cheap as brass.

a   Mexican food is spicy. British food is bland. (far)
b   The Mediterranean is warm. The North Sea is cold. (nothing like)
c   Summer temperatures in France are around 26°C. Summer temperatures in Britain are around 24°C. (only slightly)
d   Extreme sports are exciting. Racket sports are boring. (a great deal)
e   This exercise is quite difficult. The other exercises are less difficult. (a bit)

3 Put the sentences with *too* and *enough* into the correct order. Start with the word in bold.

a   long brilliant far was film too **The** but
b   allowed **Do** project we to time finish you think enough the have
c   carefully this through haven't enough **We** thought problem
d   much has money **The** venture invested company too into already this
e   too application **I'm** arrived be late your for to considered afraid you

4 Complete the paragraph about money with the words below.

▪   cash   fares   salary   money   change   wages   bills

There is a saying '1 .... makes the world go round' but whether this is true or not is debatable. What is perhaps true is that our style of living is dictated not by the amount of small 2 .... we have in our pocket but by our annual 3 .... , or the 4 .... we manage to earn on a regular basis. Without those, we wouldn't be able to pay the 5 .... , or afford the 6 .... to get us to work. And if we have nothing in the bank, the 7 .... dispenser is of little use.

5 Combine the two sentences in a–e beginning with the words given.

a   James finished cooking dinner. His sister arrived.
    No sooner ....
b   I used to trust my friend Jane. I'll never do that again.
    Under no circumstances ....
    ....
c   The plane landed on the narrow runway. All the passengers began to cheer.
    Scarcely ....
d   Central Park is beautiful. You won't find a park like this anywhere else in the city.
    Nowhere ....
e   There was a cry of protest from the audience. The politician mentioned taxes.
    Only when ....

6 Complete the dialogues using a suitable three-part phrasal verb in the correct form.

1 A: Do you want to help out at my nephew's birthday party tomorrow?
B: Sorry, but I just don't .... doing anything energetic at the moment.

2 A: Is there anyone you really .... ?
B: Yes – my grandfather. He's taught me so much about life and has lots of good advice.

3 A: So how was the trip? Did you enjoy yourself?
B: It was ok, but to be honest studying abroad didn't .... my hopes.

4 A: Why did that lovely café close down?
B: Well, I .... the waiter. He was so rude.

5 A: Did you know that Tom and Teresa had split up?
B: It doesn't surprise me. I don't know how she .... him for so long.

7 Put the verbs in brackets into the correct form to make suitable conditional sentences.

a Tim often wish he .... (join) the navy instead of going to work in a bank.

b I wish I .... (speak) Chinese.

c If only the children .... (stop) making so much noise!

d Supposing I .... (tell) you the truth – do you think you would have believed me?

e If I .... (not/drive) so fast the accident might never have happened!

f The meeting will take place unless something unforeseen .... (happen).

8 Write a synonym or explanation for each expression with *set*.

a My sister got a beautiful ring for her birthday – it's a ruby *set* in pearls.

b I'm reading a fascinating novel which is *set* in the eighteenth century.

c The team *sets* high standards for its existing and potential members.

d We haven't *set* a date for our holiday, but it will probably be sometime in June.

9 Complete sentences a–g with *so* or *such*.

a 'Is there any coffee left in the cupboard?'
'I don't think ....'

b The restaurant, ... as it was, closed down last month.

c It was .... an easy exam that I'm sure I've passed!

d Bill reached for a glass on the top shelf. As he did .... , he knocked over a vase.

e My best friend's just bought a new mobile phone. And .... have I.

f We went on holiday out of season .... we could save some money.

g This is .... a complicated instruction manual that I can't understand anything.

10 Choose the correct word to complete sentences a–f.

a The company's representative *denied/refused* to comment on the allegations of fraud.

b Please *ensure/assure* that you switch off your car alarm before leaving your vehicle.

c The results of the research were *declined/refuted* by experts in the medical field.

d Investigators are still trying to *assure/ascertain* the cause of the plane crash.

e The children *denied/rejected* all knowledge of the broken window.

f Ron *secured/assured* his boss that he would do his best to meet the deadline.

Writing

This writing section contains twelve practice tasks for Paper 2 of the CAE exam.

Each task practises the same task presented in the Student's Book and, in most cases, shares the same topic.

For help with the tasks, look back at the Student's Book and refer to the:

- **Writing** section and **How to do it** boxes in the corresponding unit
- **Writing Guide** on pages 155–164 for model answers and phrase banks

The **Vocabulary** and **Grammar** sections in the Student's Book and the Workbook will help you use a broad range of structures and vocabulary.

Unit 1 Part 2 A formal letter (character reference)

A friend of yours has decided to apply for the job described below and has asked you to write a character reference for him/her.

Write your **character reference** explaining why your friend would be suitable for the job.

Social Programme Organiser

A well-established language school for international students is looking for someone to organise and run a social programme for students during their free time. If you are:

- energetic
- resourceful
- organised

you may be just the person we need.

Unit 2 Part 2 A proposal

You are on a committee planning a festival in your town. Write a proposal saying what could be included in the festival to best represent your town, and explaining why you think your suggestions would appeal both to local people and visitors.

Write the **proposal**.

Unit 3 Part 1 A formal letter

Your student committee at college has received a memo from the Principal regarding a large sum of money recently made available to the college. You have carried out a survey into what the students think the money should be spent on. You have been asked to write a letter to the Principal telling her about the results. Use the survey results and the Principal's memo with your comments to write the **letter**.

SURVEY RESULTS

We asked students what the money should be spent on.

The results were:

Improving college sports facilities (38%)

Fund for students to take a gap year after leaving college (52%)

Providing new computers throughout the college (10%)

MEMO

TO: The student committee

FROM: M. Wright, Principal

good!

We are fortunate enough to have received a large donation of money and are keen to find out what the students think the money should be spent on. One priority might be new computers and software. *— see survey results*

no support for this from students —

Other ideas might be to build a new library, improve sports facilities, *— some support* or, more controversially, provide money for students wishing to take a year off before starting work. The final decision on how the money will be spent will be made by the board of governors. *— unfair – why ask us?!*

hardly! A great idea!

Thank you for your help in this matter.

Unit 4 Part 2 A leaflet

An international organisation called 'Back to Nature' has asked you to write an information leaflet about how people can both appreciate and protect the countryside near where you live. You should include details of interesting places nearby and how people can enjoy visiting them responsibly.

Write the **leaflet**.

Unit 5 Part 1 A letter

While studying in England, you spent a weekend with English friends at a caravan site. The site did not live up to your expectations. Read the extract from the site administrator's letter, and the publicity leaflet on which you have made some comments. Then write a **letter** to the administrator explaining what you found satisfactory and why you were disappointed, and include some suggestions for improvements.

> We were sorry to hear that your stay was not as good as you expected. Perhaps you could let us know why, and how you think the site could be improved.
>
> Yours sincerely,
>
> *Sally Thomas*
>
> Site administrator

SEAVIEW CARAVAN SITE

LOCATION

yes, but view hidden by trees

Situated in a stunning location, the site is close to the beach and within easy reach of a busy town. *not much nightlife for tourists*

ACCOMMODATION

plenty of space *didn't work!*

Spacious caravans accommodate up to six guests. All have TV, shower and separate WC, kitchenette, and a sitting area. *true* Attractively decorated throughout.

ON-SITE ACTIVITIES

always busy

A large sports hall, tennis courts and indoor swimming pool are available for the use of guests.

RESTAURANT

not for vegetarians! *good value for money*

Our on-site restaurant caters for all tastes and includes a fast-food menu.

Unit 6   Part 2 A magazine contribution

An international magazine has asked you to write an article about a well-known fictional character from your country's history. You should mention:

- when and where this character lived
- what he or she is particularly famous for
- how he or she is remembered today

Write your **magazine contribution**.

Unit 7   Part 2 A competition entry

You have seen this leaflet announcing a competition in your college.

Competition

Win a day's visit to a well-known national newspaper and find out what it takes to be a top journalist. Just write 250 words on the following subject.

What do you consider to be the greatest problem facing the world today and what can be done about it?

Write your **competition entry**.

Unit 8   Part 2 A magazine article

An international magazine for students has asked readers for articles about the best and worst inventions of recent times. You should describe your favourite and least favourite invention, and say why you have chosen them.

Write your **article**.

There has recently been an increase in the number of crimes reported by students at your college. You are the representative on the committee for student security. Read the memo from the Principal and the poster outlining safety advice for students, with the comments from students below. Then, using the information provided, write the **report** as instructed by the Principal.

No one reads posters – why not get a police officer in to give a talk?

BE SAFE AND SECURE

New students should get a leaflet reminding them to be careful.

Lock it up: most burglaries happen because doors or windows have been left open – always lock your accommodation when you leave.

Expensive to use taxis at night – how about a free college bus?

Safety in numbers: go out in groups at night, and take a taxi home rather than walking home alone.

Money matters: always keep your cash and bank cards safe in a bag or pocket.

As students we simply can't afford to lose money!

Hardly anyone has a car – more spaces for bikes please!

Car safety: always lock your car and keep valuables out of sight.

Bike sense: lock or chain your bicycle – why not have it marked with your name and postcode?

Will the college pay for us to have our bicycles marked properly?

Close call: keep your mobile phone with you but don't leave it where others can see it.

I've had my phone stolen more than once – so have most of my friends.

MEMO

TO: Representative for student security

FROM: Mary Wood, Principal

Re: Student safety

We have recently seen a significant rise in the number of crimes reported by our students. We would like to raise student awareness of the need to be safe and secure at all times. Could you get student feedback on the most important security issues and write me a report outlining:

- what students are most concerned about
- how the college can help students be safe and secure
- what else we can do to make students think about personal security

Unit 10   Part 2 A report

You have been asked to write a report for an international company about employment in your country. Your report should say:

- which jobs are most popular with young people in your country and why
- how this compares to attitudes in your parents' generation
- what companies can do to make jobs more attractive to young people

Write your **report**.

Unit 11   Part 2 A review

An international student magazine has asked you to write a review recommending two popular television programmes in your country – one for teenagers and the other for people with a special interest. You should comment on the content and style of each programme, explaining why they are suitable for each group.

Write your **review**.

You are a member of a student committee at an international college. The college is planning its annual environmental open day and the Principal has asked the student committee for their suggestions. Read the memo from the college principal and the leaflet for last year's open day, on which you have made some notes. Then, using the information given, write an **email** to staff and a **proposal** for the Principal.

MEMO

TO: Student Committee

FROM: College Principal

Re: Environmental Open Day

Our annual environmental open day is coming up on 22nd and I'd appreciate your suggestions for how we can make it the best one so far. I'm enclosing the leaflet for last year's as a reminder. Could you write me a proposal saying what wasn't so popular last year, what we should do the same, and giving some completely new ideas? Could you also send an email to staff reminding them about the open day and what its purpose is.

Jenny Ward

Principal

ANNUAL GREEN OPEN DAY

Have fun and help save the environment!
All welcome!

organised litter tidy-up
   great fun and really worthwhile!

sale of home-made vegetarian food
   delicious – why not sell the recipes?

world music stage
   two local bands – hardly world music!

guest speakers
   interesting but too old – how about some younger ones?!

book stall
   popular – include CDs and DVDs too?

theatre group
   fantastic! more of this please

solar-powered cinema
   brilliant idea but no good if it rains!

Speaking

This Speaking section reviews what you are required to do in the exam and what examiners are looking for. You will listen to CAE students doing Paper 5 Speaking tasks with CAE examiners and under exam conditions. The tasks are taken from the Student's Book and the photos are reproduced here.

The accompanying activities will help you become familiar with the format and requirements of each section. You will be able to assess the students' performances and use these as a model for practising the same tasks yourself.

Listen to the recordings as many times as necessary to do the task.

Quick quiz

1 Does the Speaking Paper carry the same marks as the other Papers?

2 How long is the test? a 10 minutes   b 15 minutes   c 20 minutes

3 Which parts of the test are being described in a–d?

   a Talk on your own about visual prompts.   Part ....
   b Discuss a problem-solving task based on visual and/or
      written prompts.   Part ....
   c Ask and answer 'personal' questions.   Part ....
   d Discuss issues related to the previous section.   Part ....

4 Now match each of the parts to the abilities that they test.

   a Discuss, evaluate, speculate and/or select.   Part ....
   b Talk about issues of general interest and express opinions.   Part ....
   c Describe, speculate, compare, contrast, comment, identify
      and eliminate.   Part ....
   d Use general interactional and social language.   Part ....

5 Complete the gaps in a–d to show what the examiners assess you on.

   a G.............. and V.............. (accurate and appropriate use of a range of
      structures and lexis)
   b D.............. M.............. (relevant comments of an appropriate length –
      long or short – and coherent expression of ideas)
   c P.............. (individual sounds, stress, rhythm and intonation)
   d I.............. Communication (sensitivity to turn-taking, appropriate
      response and initiation, speaking without undue hesitation)

Quick quiz – key

1 Yes. Each paper is worth 20%.
2 b
3 a 2, b 3, c 1, d 4
4 a Part 3   c Part 2
   b Part 4   d Part 1
5 a Grammar, Vocabulary
   b Discourse Management
   c Pronunciation
   d Interactive

Part 1

1 a Which of these questions would you expect to hear in Part 1?

> Where were you born?   Where are you from?
> How long have you been studying English?   What do you do in your country?
> What are your plans for the future?   What's your favourite time of year?

   b What answer would you give to the questions in a?

2 🎧 Listen to two extracts from Part 1 and tick the questions (in 1a) the candidates are asked. What mistakes do the candidates make?

3 a What is the procedure for the rest of Part 1? Put these activities in the correct order.

   ☐ Candidates ask each other a question prompted by the examiner.
   ☐ The examiner introduces Part 2.
   ☐ The examiner asks each candidate another direct question.

   b 🎧 Listen and check your answer to a.

   c 🎧 Listen again. Which candidate (female or male) uses better Grammar and Vocabulary and better Discourse Management?

4 What answer would you give to these questions? Demonstrate your Grammar and Vocabulary and your Discourse Management.

> Do you think that having a lot of free time is a good or a bad thing?
> Would you like to spend more time working in another country?

Part 2

1 Complete the format for Part 2 below. You have to …

   a talk about two or three .... (what?).
   b talk for .... (how long?).
   c remember to talk about all the prompts given by .... (who?).
   d answer a follow-up question after .... (who?) has finished speaking.

2 a Look at the pictures below. Make a list of vocabulary which might be useful to describe them.

   b 🎧 Listen to Alborz doing this task. Did he use any of your vocabulary? What other vocabulary did he use?

   c 🎧 Listen again. What does the examiner ask Alborz to do? Does he complete the whole task?

3 🎧 Listen to the follow-up question. How well does Yui answer it?

4 🎧 Listen again to both the questions and choose two pictures. What answers would you give?

5 Look at the two sets of pictures below. Which of the following phrases could you use to describe them? Can you think of any others?

- period costume
- early civilisations
- battle re-enactment
- transport yourself into the past
- history books
- a crowd of people
- other cultures

6 🎧 Listen to two candidates talking about the pictures as part of a **shared task** (for groups of 3 as well as pairs). Do they demonstrate points a–e and therefore give a good performance?

a quickly decide which pictures to talk about
b use a range of structures and vocabulary to compare and contrast them
c keep talking despite some hesitation or problems
d answer the whole task given by the examiner
e take turns and respond appropriately for the follow-up question

7 a Read and answer this follow-up question.

    "Which way of learning about the past gives the most accurate information?"

  b 🎧 Listen to the candidates' answers. How does your answer compare with theirs? Do they manage to keep talking and provide a full answer?

Parts 3 and 4

1 Choose the correct option to complete sentences a–c about Parts 3 and 4.

a Candidates *must/don't need to* have the same opinions.
b A conclusion *should/shouldn't* be made immediately.
c The questions in Part 4 *are/are not* related to the topics in Part 3.

2 🎧 Look at the pictures below and listen to two candidates answering a task about staying fit and healthy. Decide if statements a–g are true or false.

a The candidates waste time thinking about the task before they begin.
b They interact well with one another.
c They remember and do the task.
d They discuss all the pictures before making a final decision.
e They never interrupt or talk over each other.
f They use a range of vocabulary and structures.
g They manage to keep talking for the full amount of time.

3 🎧 Listen again and write down the task. Do this task with a partner.

4 What happens in Part 4? Complete sentences a–c.

The examiner will …
a ask questions related to ....
b expect you to express your ....
c not necessarily expect you to agree with your ....

5 a Look at the Part 4 questions below. What answers would you give?

❝ How else can you keep fit and healthy?
Should smoking be banned in all public places?
Some people say that fast food restaurants promote an unhealthy
diet. Do you agree? ❞

b 🎧 Now listen to the candidates answering the questions. List any useful
vocabulary they use.

6 a Read the instructions below for another Part 3 task and look at the pictures.
What answer would you give to this task?

❝ Here are some pictures showing decisions we sometimes have to make in
our lives.
Talk together about how difficult it is to make decisions like these, and decide
which two decisions have the greatest effects on our lives. ❞

b 🎧 Listen to some extracts from students doing the task in a. Identify the
techniques used by the candidates in each extract.

1 developing your partner's ideas   Extract ....
2 making a comment and encouraging your partner to speak   Extract ....
3 not dominating the conversation   Extract ....
4 demonstrating a range of vocabulary   Extract ....

7 🎧 Now listen to candidates doing Parts 3 and 4 of the task and list the questions
they are asked in Part 4. How would you answer these questions?

A complete test

Go to www.oup.com/elt/exams and listen to two candidates doing a complete test. Choose an activity from 1–3 below. Then, at another time in your course, choose a different activity and listen again.

The pictures for Part 2 are on page 92 and below, and the pictures for Part 3 are on page 95.

Look back at the Quick Quiz or the previous activities if you need help.

1 a Describe the procedure for each part of the Paper 5 Speaking exam.
 b Make a list of useful advice to remember for each part.
 c 🎧 Now listen to the test. Do the candidates follow the advice?

2 a What four things do the examiners assess candidates on?
 b 🎧 Now listen to the test. Use your assessment guide to rate the candidates' performances in these different areas.

3 a 🎧 Listen and stop the recording after the examiners' questions.
 b What answer would you give to each question? Use the pictures to think about useful vocabulary and ideas to discuss. Practise answering the tasks.
 c 🎧 Now listen to the candidates' answers. Did they use any of your vocabulary or ideas?

Part 2

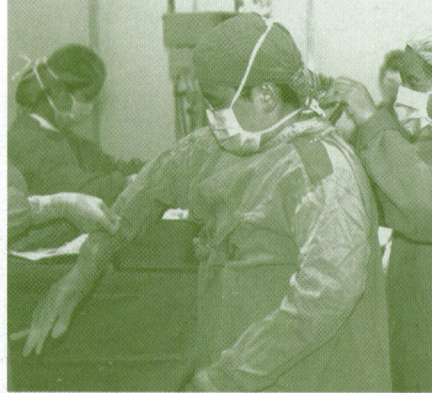